LOVE IS A STORY

LOVE IS

A NEW THEORY OF RELATIONSHIPS

ROBERT J. STERNBERG, PH.D.

OXFORD UNIVERSITY PRESS

New York   Oxford

A STORY

Oxford University Press

Oxford   New York
Athens Auckland Bangkok Bogotá Buenos Aires Calcutta
Cape Town Chennai Dar es Salaam Delhi Florence Hong Kong Istanbul
Karachi Kuala Lumpur Madrid Melbourne Mexico City Mumbai
Nairobi Paris São Paulo Singapore Taipei Tokyo Toronto Warsaw

and associated companies in

Berlin   Ibadan

Library of Congress Cataloging-in-Publication Data
Sternberg, Robert J.
    Love is a story / Robert J. Sternberg.
        p.   cm.
    Includes bibliographical references and index.
    ISBN 0-19-510642-3
    ISBN 0-19-513102-9 (Pbk.)
    1. Love.   2. Love—Case studies.   I. Title
BF575.L8S7756   1997
    152.4'1–dc21   97-43758

1 3 5 7 9 10 8 6 4 2

Printed in the United States of America
on acid-free paper

To Alejandra

~ CONTENTS

≈ PREFACE

Like everyone else, I've spent a lot of time trying to figure out why some of my close relationships have succeeded and others have failed. Like many other people, I've read about relationships, seen various media presentations about them, and gone to counselors who promised to help me understand. I've even spent a portion of my career as a psychologist trying to understand what has worked for me and what hasn't. Curiously, even my own theories didn't seem to give me the understanding I was seeking—either of my own relationships or of other people's.

I started studying love in the early 1980s, focusing initially on its structure. Together with a graduate student, Susan Grajek, I proposed a psychometric type of theory of love.[1] The goal was to discover if love could be understood in terms of its structural building blocks, and if so, to discover the nature of these building blocks. According to that theory, love could be understood in terms of a large number of disparate emotions, thoughts, and motivations—things like caring for another person, communicating well, and being supportive. The problem was that this set of "building blocks" seemed to describe elements of love, but without systematizing them and without suggesting why I or anyone else would love some people but not others.

By the late 1980s, I had proposed a new, triangular theory of love, according to which love could be understood as comprising three components: intimacy, passion, and commitment.[2] Different kinds of love would comprise different combinations of these components. For example, romantic love was characterized by intimacy plus passion, fatuous or foolish love by commitment fueled only by passion, and consummate or complete love by the combination of all three components—intimacy, passion, and commitment. Although this theory systematized kinds of love in a way that the earlier theory did not, it still did not explain why I, or anyone else, would fall in love or be able to maintain a loving relationship with one person but not another.

By the middle of the 1990s, I was seeing things in a new light. I realized that I needed to understand and systematize the many stories I had heard about relationships. These stories differed widely, not only between relationships, but sometimes within relationships: Two partners might have totally different stories about their relationship, and when the stories were very different, the partners seemed less satisfied. So I began to formulate the view of love as a story.[3] That is the view I present here. The basic idea is that we tend to fall in love with people whose stories are the same as or similar to our own, but whose roles in these stories are complementary to ours. Thus, they are like us in some ways, but potentially unlike us in others. If we happen to fall in love with someone whose stories are quite different, our relationship and the love underlying it are both at risk.

We have collected some data to test the love-is-a-story view, which are described in this book, but our validation efforts are still ongoing, as they are likely to be for a long time. Thus, this book reports a work in progress rather than a final statement of a fully tested theory.

I have written this book for everyone who is interested in love, and that probably includes just about everyone. It's not a how-to book, and it's not a book that panders to a recovery kind of mentality. I've tried to write a serious yet accessible work that may be of value to laypersons and professionals alike. I hope it presents them with a view of love that will answer questions that traditional theories—including my own previous ones—have been unable to answer, such as why we fall in love with the people we do and why we maintain love for some people but not for others.

A number of people have contributed both directly and indirectly to this book. My early collaborators in my research on love, Susan Grajek and Michael Barnes, both played a part in the development of my thinking. More recently, my collaborations with Anne Beall have also helped me further develop my ideas about love, especially with regard to how it is socially constructed.[4]

Mahzad Hojjat has been an invaluable collaborator in developing the inventory items presented in this book for assessing people's stories about love. Hojjat also collaborated in the validation of the theory, including a study in which members of a large psychology class recounted stories of their love relationships. Neil Wechsler has also been invaluable in the collection and presentation of the stories reported in this book, and in suggesting the teacher-student story.

I am grateful to all these collaborators for their work with me at various stages of the development of my work on love. Sai Durvasula put in many hours of word processing, for which I am also grateful. Finally, I am grateful to Joan Bossert for acquiring the book for Oxford University Press, to Sue Warga for copyediting the manuscript, to Kim Torre-Tasso for bringing the book into production at Oxford University Press, and to all the members of my family, who have taught me so much about love.

The stories in this book are based either on actual individual cases or on combinations of cases developed over the course of many years. However, all names and details of the cases have been changed to render them completely anonymous.

R. J. S.
New Haven, Conn.
August 1997

I THE STORIES WE TELL

What does it mean for love to be a story? What are the characteristics of stories? How do stories develop? These are the questions addressed in this part. I will show you what love stories are, why they are important, and how understanding them can change your life.

LOVE AS A STORY

Zach and Tammy have been married for twenty-eight years. Their friends have been predicting divorce for the entire time, and their predictions seem sensible. Tammy constantly threatens to leave Zach; he, in turn, lashes out at her and tells her that nothing would make him happier.

Zach and Tammy fight almost continually, and are something of an embarrassment to their friends, because the fighting is as loud as it is public. Their friends can't imagine a more ill-matched couple and have decided that the only thing that could possibly be holding Zach and Tammy together is sheer inertia.

Valerie and Leonard, on the other hand, are divorced. No one who knows them seems quite able to figure out why. They seemed to have a perfect marriage. Of course, so do many others who merely hide the problems and the pain that they feel within their relationship. But the odd thing here is that Valerie and Leonard, too, thought they had a perfect marriage. They told each other as much, and said the same to their friends. Their children have since commented that their parents virtually never fought, and that even when they did fight, the fights were more in the way of minor disagreements.

Ultimately, Valerie and Leonard split when Leonard met someone at his office and left Valerie for her. Leonard was somewhat embarrassed and ashamed of his own behavior, and could justify it only on the basis of his finally having found true love. But he admitted that before boredom set in, he had once thought Valerie to be his true love. At last count he was in therapy trying to figure out what was going on.

By the conventional wisdom, Zach and Tammy should have been splitsville, and Valerie and Leonard should have stayed married happily ever after. Their destinies seem to fly in the face of any reasonable prediction, regardless of the theory from which one makes the predictions. Might there be some way of understanding what happened to these two couples?

LOVE STORIES

One way of understanding these couples' behavior is to consider what kind of story each partner has about what love is in their current relationship and about what love ideally should be. A couple's stories of what love is and what it should be may or may not coincide. I wondered whether a couple's survival could depend on whether their individual stories of what love ideally should be were close enough to the stories of the actual relationship they were in. For example, if someone wants to live a romantic fairy tale, but finds herself actually living a war story, she is likely to be dissatisfied. Others prefer the war story, and would feel bored out of their minds in the romantic fairy tale.

What is interesting about Zach and Tammy is that both had stories that viewed love as war. No matter how bizarre or even ridiculous their relationship might seem to other people, the relationship worked for them. It corresponded well to what each of them wanted, and they both wanted the same thing. In contrast, Valerie and Leonard had a relationship that looked good to other people, but it didn't end up matching Leonard's story about what he wanted; ultimately, what he wanted and what Valerie wanted were quite different. They grew up with and still have very different stories about love.

We all grew up on love stories. Years ago, when I was much younger, Erich Segal wrote a best-selling novel and called it, very simply, *Love Story.* The title was apt—and the book was a huge success in the bookstores and on the screen. Are our real-life relationships influenced by stories such as this one?

We are often told we have to be realistic—to separate the stories we tell ourselves from what's actually going on, to distinguish fact from fiction. The whole point in getting to know someone better is supposedly to find out what the person is "really like," to go beyond what we perceive or imagine the person to be like.

But a clean separation of fact from fiction simply isn't possible in the context of personal relationships, because we shape the facts of a relationship to conform to our personal fictions. In many ways, we are a composite of our stories. As Immanuel Kant pointed out in *The Critique of Pure Reason,* if there is an objective reality, it is unknowable. All we can know is the reality we construct. That reality takes the form of a story.

Love really is a story, then—only we, rather than William Shakespeare or Gabriel García Marquez or Erich Segal or Barbara Cartland, are the authors.[1] Stories about love have existed throughout the ages, and the basic themes and plots of these stories have changed little. What has changed, however, is how these stories play out in day-to-day living, as well as the popularity of some stories compared with others. We relate better to love stories—whether in novels, plays, soap operas, or elsewhere—than we do to the self-help books or magazine articles containing lists of generic steps we are supposed to take to understand and improve our relationship. So perhaps we should be paying more attention to the love stories in our lives and less to these logically prescribed step-by-step lists. The problem with the lists is not that they aren't rational; it's that they just don't work, even if they are presented as part of a course of psychotherapy.

Conventional therapies to improve people's love lives don't work if they address only the *effects* of the stories we tell ourselves—in other words, our understanding of why the relationship failed. We need to look at the stories themselves.[2] People can go from one therapist to another, one marriage counselor to another, and find things getting no better. That's because what are being treated are symptoms rather than causes, much the way an aspirin treats the symptoms rather than the cause of an illness. An aspirin may lower the fever associated with a virus, but it won't cure a person of the virus. What's worse, the fever associated with a virus is not caused by the virus, in any case. It's a reaction of the body, which is attempting to raise its temperature in order to kill off the virus. In treating only symptoms, therefore, we may actually make things worse.

In the case of a relationship, symptoms of failure—whether they be depression, agitation, or anxiety—are signs that something is wrong. Receiving psychotherapy or taking pills may alleviate the symptoms of depression or anxiety without doing anything at all to improve the relationship that is causing the problem. We may end up tolerating a relationship that continues to be wrong for us—one that is a bad match for our own personal ideal love story—when what we really need to do is either change our relationship or change our story.

The movie *When Harry Met Sally* was quite successful when it appeared because it explored the idea of love stories and especially how stories about love differ from those concerning friendship. Harry's relationship with Sally and his perceptions of her fit into his preconceived notion of a story not about love, but about friendship. Despite their close relationship, Harry spent many years seeking romance from other women. He ultimately changed his story about love, in part because of his relationship with Sally. But until this story changed, Harry could not view Sally in a romantic way, no matter what either of them did. When Harry changed his story, his relationship with Sally improved and even transformed itself.

People will always be romantically involved, and so there will always be people trying to understand, improve, and transform their intimate relationships. People go to great lengths to do so: They talk to one another, to friends outside the relationship, to family members, and to therapists. They buy books, attend courses, and watch videos. But how successful are people in their attempts to make their relationships work? The divorce rate, which in the United States and many other countries hovers around 50 percent, gives us a clue, but only a limited one. We can all think of relationships that will probably not break up but are nevertheless unhappy. Most of us can count on one hand the relationships we know that really *are* happy.

Either intimate connections are impossibly difficult or, somehow, our attempts at understanding and improving relationships are failing to take into account an important aspect of what goes into maintaining them. This is where the idea of love as a story can be helpful: Each of us has an ideal story about love, and it may be the most important thing we can learn about ourselves.

RELATIONSHIPS AS STORIES

When we first meet someone, we naturally want to get to know that person better, to see whether they think the way we do. We want to match up our first impressions with realities, to substitute fact for fiction, truths for stories. We imagine, in getting to know someone, that we replace a "fiction" with the "reality" of nonfiction. But if we think about first impressions, about the rituals surrounding mating and marriage, this replacement is often not what really happens. We come to relationships with many preconceived ideas. These ideas, or stories, are not right or wrong in themselves, although they may be more or less adaptive—that is, more or less healthy in promoting a good fit to the environment. What is viewed as adaptive varies over time and place. For example, one culture might view love as an indispensable part of marriage; another culture might view love as irrelevant to marriage. In both cultures, these values are likely to be taught not as somewhat arbitrary matters of cultural convention, but as matters of right and wrong. What are viewed as "realities" are rather perceptions of realities—stories. The story gives the relationship meaning in the context of our lives. Sometimes each partner in a relationship sees different meaning in the same actions or events, because each interprets the actions or events in terms of a different story.

My Story, Your Story

When Tyrone met Samantha, he thought he had found the love of his life. He had made mistakes before, but not this time. Samantha seemed to have everything he was looking for, even things he had thought he would never find. She was beautiful, smart, sexy, out-going, poised, and interested in sports, and she had a good sense of humor. Best of all, she was interested in him. Tyrone suggested to Samantha that they go to a Cubs game together; she accepted.

Within a month Tyrone and Samantha were dating steadily. In two months they were an item. After three months Tyrone was beginning to have second thoughts. He was pretty sure that Saman-tha was seeing at least one other man on the sly, maybe more than one. The whole story was beginning to have a ring of ugly familiarity to it—a woman who can't be trusted, who pretends to be true but cheats the first chance she gets. Tyrone was glad that he had gotten to know Samantha better, before it was too late. After some ugly scenes, the relationship came to a bitter end. Tyrone was glad it had; so was Samantha, who hadn't been seeing anyone besides Tyrone and didn't want to be with a man whom she had come to view as delusional.

While Tyrone may seem delusional, perpetually imagining that his partners are cheating on him, in a sense we are all like Tyrone. As we begin to get to know people, we start to project our own thoughts and feelings—the wisdom we've acquired as well as the emotional baggage of our past—onto them. As a result, though we feel we are getting to know a person more intimately, we may not really be doing that at all. On the contrary, we may be creating a story that has less and less to do with what the person is really like, and more to do with what we *imagine* that person to be like. Indeed, we know people only through our own perceptions of them.

You're not like Tyrone, you say. Perhaps you are more like him than you realize. I was once talking to a famous love researcher about his relationship with his wife. This individual is a leader in the field of close relationships, elite among those people who have sought a psychological understanding of such partnerships. He described to me how one day, after more than two decades of marriage, he was having a conversation with his wife in the living room. The fire was burning, it was twilight outside, and the setting couldn't have been more romantic. His wife made an offhand comment, and all of a sudden his whole perspective on the relationship changed. He realized that the way he was viewing the relationship and the way she was viewing it had just about nothing in common. More than twenty years, and somehow he hadn't noticed. Further conversations confirmed, at least for him, his new hypothesis. And his marriage eventually ended.

This love researcher was no Tyrone. Yet he was as susceptible to illusions as any one of us. Was his new perception correct? Really, there is no way to know for sure. Like Tyrone, he started with one story and replaced it with another. His wife, like Samantha, had her own, different story. There is no objective, "right" story of a relationship, or at least none we can know.

If you have any doubts, just talk to two people going through a divorce. As often as not, it will sound as though each of them is describing a different marriage. The relationship one partner depicts is likely to have little or nothing to do with the one the other describes. That's a major reason they're divorcing: Their stories about the relationship they are in have diverged to the point where there are virtually no points of similarity.

Divergence of stories is not limited to failing relationships, however. In collaboration with Michael Barnes, I did a study in which we asked couples to fill out questionnaires that asked how they felt about their partner and how they thought the other felt about them.[3] In some of the questions, each partner had to guess how the other partner would respond. On a scale of 0 to 1, where 0 indicated that the person just guessed at random how the partner would respond and 1 indicated that the person always guessed correctly, the correlation between how the partner actually responded and how the individual thought his or her partner would respond was a mere 0.3. In other words, there was only a modest relationship between how the individuals responded and how their partners thought they would respond. People had only the foggiest idea of how their partners really felt about them. And these were couples in stable relationships! Imagine what the results might have been for couples in failing relationships. In my experience, as often as not, when one partner indicates dissatisfaction or even asks for a divorce, the other partner feels caught totally off guard. Yet if one were to ask the partner wanting a divorce if the news was unexpected, that person would probably say that he or she had warned the other dozens, even hundreds of times. The two partners' stories about the relationship have so diverged that their communication has become largely an illusion. In contrast, relationships are more likely to succeed when common stories generate shared worldviews, assumptions about relationships, and interpretations of events—all of which form foundations for good communication.

The fact that people have different stories of love highlights an important point about love: Trying to figure out what love "is" can be a frustrating and futile effort, because it's not quite the same thing for any two people. It's a story to everyone, but what's in that story can differ widely from one person to another. At the same time, though, two people in a relationship need somehow to create a shared story in addition to their individual ones.

Our Story

Not only does each person have a personal story of the relationship, but each person also has a conception of a joint story that he or she believes the couple shares. The shared story may or may not correspond to either individual's story, and of course the two partners may have different conceptions of the shared story. Consider Beth and Blake.

Beth and Blake have been together twenty years, and both are happy in the relationship. They are proud of the fact that they have stuck it out for twenty years and that although there have been a few tensions, especially around their two children, their marriage has been relatively trouble-free. In many ways, they are the model of the happy couple. Maybe not in every way, though.

Beth has been seeing David for six months, almost seven. David is divorced and is not interested in remarrying. Curiously, leaving Blake is one of the last things Beth could imagine doing. She really is happy with him, but in a tranquil and somewhat unexciting kind of way. She finds that seeing David generates a kind of excitement in her life that she just doesn't get with Blake.

Beth feels guilty over her relationship with David. She knows it doesn't make any real sense, and what's more, if Blake found out, he would be out the door in a minute. There would be no reconciliation—not for Blake. He is just too proud. One part of her wants to terminate the relationship with David right away, before it's too late. But another part of her—which seems to exist in parallel with the first—just can't seem to let go.

Beth has a curious ambivalence about the whole situation. Her actual story about her relationship with Blake is a positive one. Their shared story is also very positive, but what, exactly, is that shared story? She knows that Blake's conception of that shared story and hers can't be the same. When she is with Blake, she knows she is pretending. The actual story with Blake is just too far from her ideal story. Sooner or later, something's got to give. Beth is not sure what it will be.

The case of Beth and Blake was actually more complex than it appeared, because, unbeknownst to Beth, Blake was also seeing someone else, and having almost exactly the same thoughts as Beth. Had they communicated to each other their sense of the stagnation in the relationship, they might have repaired it. Instead, each sought to keep the other in the dark.

Beth and Blake both appear to be pretending, when in fact they may have more in common than they know. Sometimes the story a couple shares is so threadbare it cannot withstand the slightest of tests. A recent article in a national newspaper told of an engaged couple who had just split up over a lottery ticket. The woman bought the ticket and gave it to the man to hold. The ticket was a winner and the woman wanted it back—it was hers. The man didn't see it that way—it was theirs, and he believed that the man manages the money. Now it's a matter for the courts to decide. The couple discovered, too late, that their views on relationships were not very much alike.

It is often said that with time partners become more alike. Part of the reason for this perception is that people not only attempt to choose partners with matching stories, but also act in ways that actively shape the behavior of their partner, to make it a better match to their story. In other words, if the partner does not quite conform to the desired role, the individual will act in ways—consciously or unconsciously—intended to encourage the desired behavior on the part of the partner. The result of shaping can be that an individual finds him- or herself playing a role in a relationship that he or she before would never have imagined possible. It may or may not be an agreeable or even acceptable role for the individual. If the role is not acceptable, the individual may find the relationship to be exerting power over her that he or she does not welcome.

Relationships are powerful and transforming, changing us in ways we may not want. It is not only our love story that moves us to act, but our partner's love story as well. And the situation is complicated by the fact that each of us has multiple stories about love. How do these multiple stories play out? Are they conscious? We turn to these questions and others in the next chapter.

OUR MULTIPLE STORIES
OF LOVE

Typically, each of us has multiple stories about love, not just one. These stories underscore the fact that not only is love not quite the same thing for different people, but it is not even one simple thing for us individually. Consider the case of Aaron and Lucy.

Aaron has been seeing Lucy for seven months. It's the second time around for both of them, but they both have been acting as though this is it. They've discovered they both want the same things out of life and that they are compatible. When they're together, everything is calm and relaxed—at last. Both came from contentious marriages that almost never allowed them to be calm or relaxed. What a change! They are starting to talk marriage and children— a life together. Conversations that started out as about a hypothetical future somehow have become about what now seems like a real future. Lucy isn't quite sure how the speculations so quickly transformed themselves into something more. It just seemed to happen.

Unfortunately, other things were also happening. Three weeks ago, Aaron wouldn't have cared about Dottie. Now he is thinking that maybe he does care after all. On a week-long business trip, he met Dottie, an assistant manager at the plant he was visiting. As the week went on, it seemed to become more a story about Dottie than about the business trip. He started off trying to sell her machine parts, and ended up trying to sell her himself. Aaron is totally confused.

He has a good relationship with Lucy. He wasn't looking for another relationship. On the contrary, he viewed Lucy and himself as a serious couple. They are both serious people, and they have found a life together without the hassles and stresses of their prior marriages. Keeping the relationship hassle-free is something they have made a point of. His evolving relationship with Dottie isn't anything like that at all. If anything, it is more like the relationship he had in the marriage he has now put behind him. He should be running away from Dottie as fast as his legs can carry him; but his legs aren't running, definitely not.

The relationship with Dottie is fun, most of the time, and not very serious at all. But when there's a fight—and there already have been two—it's a doozy, leaving Aaron tense and unable to function well. Aaron thinks he's nuts to be involving himself with Dottie, but he keeps going back for more.

Aaron hasn't mentioned Lucy to Dottie, or Dottie to Lucy, for that matter. At the end of the week, he figures, he's going to have to make some sort of decision. He's either got to break it off with Dottie or with Lucy, or adjust his relationship with one or the other of them, or something else he hasn't thought of yet. The one thing he knows is that he doesn't want to get into a situation where he has two relationships going in two different cities. He feels like a heel. He can't understand how he could be attracted to both Lucy and Dottie—they're just so different from each other. But he knows he's attracted to both of them.

Eventually Aaron broke off with Dottie and returned to Lucy. But soon thereafter, the relationship with Lucy broke up as well. It didn't really work for either Aaron or Lucy. For both of them, it was an attempt to distance themselves as much as they could from their former relationships. But going from one extreme to the other usually doesn't work. It is a strategy for avoiding the past rather than for confronting the future.

Aaron's situation is not unusual. All of us have more than one story that we seek to reconcile in our love relationships. Usually we are not conscious of what these stories are, nor are we conscious that our stories carry different weights in how they affect us. In other words, there will be some stories we prefer over others. Different partners bring out different stories in us.

As a result, what we accept at one point as a satisfactory or even good love relationship may rather quickly appear inadequate if another potential partner can begin to play a role in another story higher in our preference hierarchy. When we meet a new potential partner who corresponds to a story higher in our hierarchy, the old partner may all of a sudden lose much of his or her attractiveness. It even can be embarrassing how fast someone who appeared attractive one moment could appear relatively unattractive the next. Such changes can come about when we are unaware of our hierarchy of stories and the effect it has on us.

Because we are usually unaware of the contents of our preferences, or even that we have such a hierarchy, we may be as surprised as anyone when we find ourselves reexamining a current relationship from an entirely new vantage point. This is what happened to Aaron. Both women appealed to him because each could play a role in one of his stories. Aaron was finding himself confused as to what he wanted.

Actually, Aaron wanted both love stories, but he didn't want to have two relationships simultaneously. So he, like most of us, had to choose one of them, or neither. Aaron is probably lucky that neither relationship ultimately worked out, because neither relationship produced a story that fully satisfied him.

The same thing happened to Leonard in the vignette mentioned earlier. Valerie initially seemed to be a match for what Leonard had thought he wanted out of a love relationship. Leonard had thought Valerie was what he wanted, until he discovered someone else whose story was even closer to his ideal. Of course, he may yet meet someone even closer to his ideal, or he might change his ideal story. At some point, we all either have to decide that what we have is close enough, or risk a string of very short-term relationships.

MOUNTAIN CLIMBING

Imagine yourself at the bottom of a mountain. You want to climb to the top, but it's dark, and cloudy to boot, so you can't see the top of the mountain, or even very far along the path you are climbing. The only way you can climb the mountain is to feel with your foot all around where you are, and make the step that will take you higher. You've got to keep the steps small, however, lest you take a big step and accidentally fall off.

So you climb the mountain slowly, not really sure where you are going. Eventually you reach a peak—everywhere you place your foot, it is lower than where you are now. There is nowhere to go now but down. So you must be at the top of the mountain, right? Wrong.

You don't really know if you have reached the top of the mountain. You may have just reached the highest spot on that path, but not the summit of the mountain as a whole. Because it's dark, though, you can't even know whether the peak you have reached is just a local peak or the ultimate summit. You may be trapped on a relatively low peak, thinking that you have reached the top. Everywhere near to you is a descent, but for all you know, just a quarter mile away may be a path up to a much higher peak.

You now have two options. You can decide that you've climbed high enough and stay where you are. Or you can descend to some other point on the mountain and start the whole process all over again, hoping that you can find a higher peak. You may find a higher peak, or you may not. There's just no way of knowing for sure. So you have to decide whether you want to take the risk. At best, you find a higher peak, still not knowing whether it is the summit. At worst, you never find a peak as high as the one you are now on. In other words, you may never again get even as high as you currently are.

So it is with stories of love. You never really know whether the relationship you are in and the story it represents are the best you can find. Maybe there's a better story waiting for you. Or maybe there is a better representation of the story you are now in. In other words, a relationship with another person might appeal to another story you hold dear, or it might be a better version of the same love story you are now in. Just as the mountain climber in the dark and fog cannot be sure where he or she stands, in love most of us feel as if we have been left in the dark. Our partners are also in the dark. This leaves both of us uncertain about what is what—about what is "true."

The Relationship Between Stories and Events

Couples often argue about whose view better represents the "truth," but from the love-is-a-story standpoint, it is difficult, if not impossible, to know any truth about a relationship. This is because the information the partners have, as well as the information they give to others, is always filtered through their stories about their relationships. Two partners may each be convinced that the other is lying when in fact each is telling the truth as he or she sees it.

Consider, for example, a common problem in relationships between men and women. Dean's idea of a loving relationship is one that is smooth, tranquil, and relatively conflict-free. If two people genuinely love each other, he thinks, they accept each other as they are, meaning that they are nonconfrontational and don't attack each other verbally. For Susan, however, two people in love confront their differences and together forge a common path. Susan believes that if a couple doesn't engage in communication, especially communication about their differences, they cannot even begin to move ahead together. The result is that Susan confronts Dean pretty much whenever she sees problems.

Dean views these confrontations as attacks, which, to his mind, are precisely what people who love each other should not initiate. He withdraws. Susan, frustrated by his withdrawal, becomes more assertive, resulting in Dean's further withdrawal, and so on. The relationship is deteriorating, not because the two people see different facts or even because they don't love each other, but because their different stories about what love should be lead them to interpret events in opposite ways. The relationship may fall apart simply because neither partner has understood the other's story about love. No matter how many experiences the partners have together, their divergent stories keep them apart.

If experiencing more events together doesn't lead to any kind of "truth," then how can we possibly get to know each other? Why even bother? Actually, there is a good reason to get to know someone better; it's just not what we usually think it is.

To get to know someone better, we can try to see our relationships as a reflection of the shared story we are in and of the role that each is playing in the shared story. As I have already pointed out, Kant long ago said that we can never know things in themselves—the ultimate essences of things. What we can get to know, however, are our perceptions of things. And as we have more experiences, these perceptions become more and more complex and rich. They do not necessarily become more valid, in an absolute sense, or even any more internally consistent. On the contrary, the more we get to know about a person, the more contradictory the person may seem to be! Of course, it may be our impressions rather than our partners themselves that are contradictory.

The notion that we can never get to know things in themselves, be it people or anything else, may seem like a depressing view. Yet it is an important notion, because it helps us realize that our relationships with people are no more subjective, in some ways, than other things we experience in life. Take colors, for example. Look at the clothing you are wearing now. What colors do you see? Where do those colors exist?

Colors, of course, appear to be in the things we see. But they're not. All that your clothing can do is absorb certain bands of electromagnetic radiation and reflect others. The interactions between the reflected bands and your eyes produce what we know as colors.[1] Some people, and many kinds of animals, are fully or partially colorblind. And for all we know, the conundrum that children often pose for each other—is the blue you see the same as the blue I see?— may have something to it. There is no way of knowing whether the cone cells in your eyes (the cells that perceive color) function in exactly the same way as the cone cells in my eyes. There just is no way of knowing whether we are all seeing the same thing as blue.

Whether we see colors in the same way is debatable. Whether people see the colors of love in the same way is not, because they don't. In the case of love, people will always interpret events in different ways. What one individual sees as constructive criticism, another will see as an attack, as in the case of Dean and Susan. What one sees as designed to save a relationship, another will see as designed to destroy it, as shown in the case of Kate and Ernest.

Kate is off to France again. Her import-export business is going well, which is lucky, because Ernest has been out of a job for six months. A victim of downsizing, he has been unable to find any kind of work that will bring him anything close to what he was making before he lost his upper-level management job in a major telecommunications company.

Ernest feels ashamed that he has not been able to find work. He is also angry, because with his thirty-three years of experience, he should be a shoo-in at the company of his choice. He thinks he is a victim of age discrimination, but he has no way to prove it. Moreover, he knows how business works, and how he has hired people in the past: Why pay more if you can get someone roughly as good for much less?

While Ernest is happy that Kate's business is going so well, he is also resentful that she never seems to be around. He knows that in the early years of the marriage, she hardly ever said a word when he was at work sixty hours a week. But they are older now, and Ernest wants Kate around more. She answers that if she doesn't travel a lot, they will be in the breadline. Kate sees her traveling as the only way to maintain the relationship, and even, of providing food and shelter.

Ernest just doesn't believe it. He suspects that Kate simply doesn't really enjoy being with him, and in retrospect, he thinks that maybe that's why she never said anything when he was always at work in the past. How differently events can be interpreted in retrospect!

What Kate sees as the only hope for saving the marriage and for keeping them out of poverty, Ernest sees as sabotage. Who's right: Kate, Ernest, both of them, or neither of them? The one thing you can say for sure is that whoever is right, both of them are feeling anxious and unsure about the future of their relationship.

One Relationship and Many Competing Stories

The story of Kate and Ernest shows that relationships involve many stories, not only of love, but of various kinds—about money, about children, about sex, and about many other things as well. People may even have stories about their stories—explaining why, for example, they feel so jealous about their partner ("I'm always worrying about where my partner is because maybe she's with another guy" or "Twenty years ago, the guy I thought was my best friend was sleeping with my wife").

People who tend to be jealous may realize that it will be difficult for them to be with someone who doesn't like to report on where or with whom he or she is spending time. That's what happened to Julio. He just needed to know where Maria was. It wasn't anything about her personally. There were a lot of positive aspects to their relationship. But Julio had to know that his wife was loyal to him, and the only way he could really be sure was to know how she was spending her time.

Maria interpreted Julio's need to know as a lack of confidence in her. Their relationship met a lot of her needs, and she enjoyed other aspects of it. But Maria didn't want to feel like she was spending her life in a prison. And more and more, that was the way she was feeling. Julio called it curiosity; she called it morbid jealousy. She wanted out. It wasn't so easy, though. Julio didn't want out, and Maria was genuinely afraid of what he would do if she left. She'd gone to counselors, a lawyer, a minister, and friends. No one seemed to be able to help her, especially because Julio really hadn't done anything illegal. She felt stuck. She was. The story that was unfolding over time just seemed to be getting worse. How do stories unfold over time, and what are the elements of these stories?

STORY ELEMENTS

O ur story about a relationship, and the elements that go with it, may change, but the story is always our story. Even if a partner helps us "write" the story, it is our creation, and the partner is likely never fully to understand what our story involves. This story is apt to have enormous staying power.

Stories do change over time, but they do not simply disappear. Rather, we endlessly elaborate old stories, and gradually replace old stories with new ones. The new stories may be better or worse, but they remain as stories nonetheless. We develop our stories as we go along, adding chapters as unanticipated events and new directions enter our lives. Retrospective stories, those we create after relationships end, reflect our attempts to incorporate hindsight into our understanding of what was going on in the relationship, and may be quite different from prospective stories, those we create before a relationship begins. After a relationship ends, we may change the narrated beginning of the story to make it a better fit with the story's end.

Stories about our relationships are like all other stories: They have beginnings, middles, and endings. These three broad stages of a story have different properties.

Beginnings are in many ways the most exciting part of stories. Who knows what will happen? Beginnings would seem to be largely a function of the person we meet: What's he or she like, and what is our reaction to him or her? We tend to underestimate the extent to which we are filling in gaps in our knowledge about a partner with expectations from our own experience. To a large extent, we are projecting the person we hope to meet onto the person we are actually meeting. Part of the excitement of the beginning of a relationship is exactly this projection onto that real person standing in front of us so much of what we hope the person will turn out to be.

Even when our relationship is only at the beginning, most of us supply an imagined ending to our present love story. Endings are always tentative, because even when relationships end, we do not close the book on them. We usually continue retrospectively to develop and embellish and sometimes to change the story that we have about a relationship. Thus a divorce may legally end a relationship, but the story goes on, and may change over time, even in the total absence of any contact with the ex-partner. Many divorced individuals will find that the story they tell themselves and others about an ended relationship is quite different ten years after the divorce than it was the day after.

Endings do not occur just at the moment when we cease to be in an intimate partnership with someone else. Because we, like authors, partially plot out our stories in advance and partially let the story writing guide itself, we may have, consciously or not, a pretty good sense of the way a relationship is going to end almost as soon as the relationship has begun, or even before it has "officially" begun. Obviously, the course of events may change our predictions, and thus how the story evolves. But our anticipation of the ending can shape the relationship as much as the relationship can shape the actual ending. The anticipated ending can determine in advance what kinds of plots and themes we will allow our story to develop.

Love stories have plots, themes, and characters. These elements, which combine aspects of the relationship with aspects of our personal history (as do the plots and themes of all story writers), are largely of our own creation.

The plot of a love story is simply what is happening in a relationship. It has both a surface level (what seems to have happened) and a deeper level (what we think really happened). One would think that plot is objective, but it isn't. For example, suppose a couple puts a down payment on a house—that much they agree on. But what did they really do? To one partner, they bought themselves a dream, a refuge. To the other, they sank their hard-earned savings into a money pit. The events that transpire after the purchase will almost certainly be seen by these two individuals in different ways.

Sometimes couples cannot even agree on the physical events, much less on their interpretations. Zach once asked Tammy who was the leading actor in a movie he remembered their having seen together, and Tammy replied by suggesting he must have gone to see the movie with someone else. The event itself is of much less significance than the plots woven around it—in this case, a plot revolving around Zach's having secret movie trysts (and who knows what other kinds of trysts) with someone besides Tammy.

Underlying the plot is a theme. The theme tells us what our stories mean. The themes are the lessons we think we are learning from what happens in a relationship. For example, in the house-purchasing example, one partner interprets the purchase as an indication that the other partner is a spendthrift; the other partner interprets the purchase as an indication that the other partner lacks any sense of a true home and refuge. But in reality, we construct these themes as much as we do the plot.

Two people could take the same events and develop completely different themes, thinking they are learning different things from the relationship. So two people may end a relationship, one forswearing serious relationships forever and the other starting to look for another serious partner right away. Both would think they have learned the lesson the relationship had to teach. The two people will now develop very differently, one perhaps never again allowing new characters to play a romantic role in his or her life.

You might think that the characters of our love stories are pretty obvious, but even here there are complications. For example, relationships, even between two people, always involve partners past and present. Our relationship with a partner is affected by other characters, past and present, some of whom we may not even be aware of. Moreover, as in literature, what makes characters who they are for us is colored by the kinds of stories we bring to our relationships. Two different people who have relationships with the same person may see that person in a totally different light, almost to the point that the only shared features are the physical ones (and even physical features may be perceived in different ways). We "construct" the people who inhabit our minds pretty much in the same way that we construct our relationships with them. For the most part, our constructions are intuitive.

Stories, like love itself, function primarily at the intuitive or experiential level. People who are really trying to improve their relationships often turn to psychologists for help. But psychologists often fail to appreciate how much love has to do with stories rather than with scientific analysis.

Love is synthetic rather than analytic—literally synthetic in the sense that we synthesize a story in the course of our experiences. Stories conform to intuitive and experiential rules, not logical and rational ones. So we need to understand our relationships as narratives, not as logical systems that need to fit. The psychologist Seymour Epstein has compared the characteristics of experiential or narrative thinking to those of rational thinking.[1] Consider what he found.

Narrative thinking tends to be holistic, intuitive, illogical, concrete, rapidly accomplished, slow to change, and self-evidently valid ("experiencing is believing"). Rational thinking, in contrast, tends to be analytic, rational, logical, abstract, more slowly accomplished, rapidly changed, and requiring justification through logic and evidence for belief. Consider the case of Brian and Sylvia.

When Brian asks Sylvia why she left him, Sylvia is able to give Brian reasons. But the reasons are clear only in retrospect. They give Brian, and to some extent Sylvia, a set of seemingly rational explanations as to why the relationship didn't work, at least from Sylvia's point of view. Communication was increasingly poor; lovemaking had become unsatisfying; the time spent together was inadequate. But those reasons were just symptoms of some underlying problem, and intuitively Sylvia knew as much at the narrative level of thinking. Why was communication increasingly poor? Why had love-making become unsatisfying?

The real reason was that, to Sylvia, as both of their careers took off, the relationship between the two of them had become more like a business story than a romance. For Sylvia, the story of a love relationship should not resemble that of a business. As a result, she found herself less able to communicate with Brian and less interested in making love to him. The story had changed from one she liked to one she didn't. Sylvia's relationship with Brian was failing because, at an intuitive, narrative level, Sylvia no longer felt herself to be in a love relationship. She didn't want a love relationship that presupposed that love is a business, not for any particular rational reason, but because it didn't feel right to her.

Often, the problem in a love relationship is not the actual thinking that people do, but the presuppositions of that thinking—the content of the stories people bring to relationships. The next chapter explores the content of stories in more detail.

SOME KINDS OF STORIES

All our lives we have heard stories of various kinds, many with love as a leitmotif. We thus have an array of stories we can draw on when composing our own. The ones we choose to carry through life reflect what interests us; they can be classified loosely according to their content, rather like the way books are grouped into various interest sections in a bookstore. These stories form the heart of this book; the second part of the text will elaborate upon them.

The current list of twenty-five stories presented here represents a wide range of conceptions of what love can be. These stories are the ones that came up over and over again in our interviews, but there are likely many more (mostly unconscious) stories that people harbor about love, and so this list should be looked on as tentative—a hint of the kinds of stories we hold. Some of the conceptions (for example, love as a garden) may seem more common than others (such as love as pornography).

Each story has a characteristic mode of thought and behavior. For example, someone who sees love as a game between two contestants will behave very differently toward a loved one than will someone who sees love as religion. The first person may see events as attributable to fate, but not the second person, who sees design underlying events. These two individuals are likely to automatically react to events in different ways.

A particular love story, with its assumptions about what a loving relationship is or should be, can operate almost in the same way as "automatic thoughts"—thoughts that just seem to come to us with no effort.[1] We may not be aware that these assumptions are idiosyncratic to our own particular story about love. Instead, we consider our assumptions to be a more or less "correct" characterization of what love is or should be, and we will often view partners who fail to measure up as being somehow inadequate. But we may also view ourselves as inadequate if we cannot conform to the roles we imagine we play in our relationships. Thus, if someone views love as a business arrangement but can't form this kind of relationship after several tries, the person may feel inadequate in loving relationships, despite the fact that he or she may be able to form a different kind of loving relationship. Sometimes, though, the person may have the right story but the wrong role within the story.

Love stories have complementary roles. We are happiest with someone who shares our story or who at least has a compatible story that can more or less fit with ours, but this someone need not be a person who is just like ourselves. Instead, we look for someone who is like us in sharing a similar story, but who is complementary to us in the role they play within that story.

Consider, for example, what I call the addiction story (described later in the book), in which one partner is addicted to the relationship and to the love underlying it. Two partners may share an addiction story, but for the relationship to work, they need to take complementary roles. One will typically be the addict; the other is the co-dependent, who "helps" the addict through his or her tribulations. The addiction may be to the partner, but may also be to drugs, alcohol, or even a cause. The critical element is the presence of addiction, and it probably matters much less exactly what it is to. Ironically, if the addict is able to conquer the addiction, the relationship may begin to fail, because the relationship is no longer sustained by the story the partners hold.

The past addict may no longer need or even want the codependent, who is a reminder of the addiction, while the codependent is without a role to play in the absence of the other's addiction. Thus, a story that works at one point in life may not work at another point, just as a story that works for one person may not work for another.

What works for one person or in one situation may not work for another person or in another situation. For example, a love story in which humor is the major theme—in which joking and seeing things in a humorous way play a major part in the love relationship—may serve to make a relationship fun and interesting for a couple, and their frequent joking may keep their relationship alive and fresh. At the same time, such joking may be used to avoid true intimacy, to cover up problems, or it may be a way of acting aggressively toward a partner in a veiled and negative way. Thus, a story that works well for the partners under some circumstances may not do so under others. To understand whether a relationship is working or not for the partners who are in it, we need to understand the story underlying the relationship.

Certain stories seem to have more potential for success than others do, but again, what makes a story potentially successful depends on the people, their situation, and the culture in which the story is embedded. How well stories work can also depend on the extent to which people believe in them.

A story can succeed only for someone who believes in it. Leonard, whose story was considered earlier, was in what would have been a perfect relationship for many people. Leonard's shared story was what I call a garden story, which generally is an adaptive one. The goal of this story is to keep the relationship and the partner well cared for, much the way one would tend the flowers in a garden. The problem was that Leonard thought he wanted this story, but there was another, ideal story that also clamored for his attention. As revealed in his subsequent relationship, Leonard's ideal story was closer to a mystery story. He wanted mystery and intrigue, but he knew Valerie like an open book. In general, the problem with mystery and intrigue is that they are usually associated with the beginning of a relationship. People who feel they need mystery in their love story sooner or later end up being disappointed. What originally caused happiness may later have unhappiness as its main effect.

Stories are both causes and effects in the way they interact with the rest of our lives. The stories we bring to relationships may cause us to behave in certain ways, and they can even elicit certain behaviors from others. At the same time, our own development and our interactions with others may shape and modify the stories we bring to our relationships, and through which we try to achieve success in these relationships.

The potential for success of any kind of story depends on how one defines success. Zach and Tammy, whose story was presented earlier, are succeeding where everyone expected them to fail because they share a story about love that sees love as a kind of war. The fact is that, behind the threats and blowups, they are happy with what they have and probably wouldn't know what to do without it. Both come from conflict-ridden households not dissimilar to the household they have produced. Is the relationship "successful"? Yes, if measured by the compatibility of their love stories. Yes, if measured by their staying together. No, if measured by their constant complaints about each other, or if the relationship were to be evaluated by the couple's verbally described satisfaction, which would be in the nether regions of any numerical scale of success. There is no unitary criterion for success. Moreover, the members of a couple may each define success differently, as may third parties viewing the relationship from afar. Different definitions of success may themselves derive from different stories.

Relationships work best when people have compatible kinds of stories. Consider the example of Jane and Don. Jane has become very unhappy in her relationship with Don. For Jane, the story of her relationship with Don is a police story. If Don doesn't like Jane's clothes, he expects Jane to change. He'll tell her she looks dumpy, or frumpy, or sloppy. Don watches what she eats, and will even countermand her order at a restaurant if he doesn't approve. Jane has finally convinced Don to let her work, but Don won't let her take a job with any remote possibility of a career track. Don's need for control is destroying the relationship, because Jane does not want to live the rest of her life like a convicted felon out on parole. There is no version of a police story that will satisfy her.

Jane's ideal story is a garden story, in which she and Don would be lovingly tending to their relationship the way a dedicated gardener would tend to a garden. Jane would probably do best with someone else who wanted to tend to the garden of a relationship. And she might do fine with someone who has a related story. For example, someone with a "cookbook" story tends to look for formulas that make relationships work, and Jane might be convinced to search for a formula to make the garden blossom. But she has no place in her life for a policeman who creates for her a jail or a life in which she feels as though she is under constant surveillance.

People write their own versions of all of the stories here, and may have altogether different stories from those described in the second part of the book. Moreover, our stories change over time. Thus, the kinds of stories considered in Part II should serve as guidelines, not as a taxonomy that is set in stone.

WHERE DO STORIES COME FROM, AND WHERE CAN THEY GO?

Where do our stories come from? We take our perceptions and construct them into what we may believe to be considered an accurate story. But our experiences, emotions, motives, and cognitions affect our stories. Our individual personality traits may also lead us to perceive things in different ways. This background serves as the basis for the themes in our stories, and it very much affects the kind of story (happy or sad, long or short, heroic or villainous) that we put together.

When we construct new stories, we often select portions of old ones and add new material to accommodate a new relationship. If we have a history of feeling rejected, we are likely to be highly sensitive about rejections, and to interpret behavior as rejecting, even if it is not intended that way. Rejection is thus likely to become a major theme of our love stories and to be woven into every plot. If we have historically mistrusted loved ones, we will be looking for signs that our current loved one is not worthy of our trust, and we are likely to fashion themes of deception into our stories, because any behavior can be interpreted in an infinite variety of ways, including as being devious. We often create what's not there. Consider the case of Allan and Dale.

Allan is an example of a man who finds the theme of rejection in almost every plot. As an adolescent, Allan really did endure painful rejections from female peers. Now he is twenty-eight, but his high-school days continue to exist inside him. If his live-in lover, Dale, is distracted one day, Allan views her distraction as a sign that she is losing interest. If she makes plans that don't involve him, Allan feels he has been purposely excluded. If Dale rejects Allan's choice of a restaurant, Allan takes it as a personal rejection of himself.

An intelligent individual, Allan often recognizes that he is responding in a less-than-rational manner. But the recognition usually doesn't help, for he feels the rejection as painfully as if Dale actually meant to reject him. Allan's own fearful story about what could happen to their love disrupts his perceptions of what's going on. He cannot see things clearly.

We all say to ourselves, from time to time, "Now I see things clearly." But we never see things independently of our stories. We are always influenced by their themes, and are better off realizing this than believing that we can somehow disregard or ignore them. The themes stem from our childhoods, from interactions with parents, siblings, and friends; they come, too, from our adolescent interactions (often the most painful ones). But they never leave us. The themes that most affect us are those from our experience that, in interaction with our personalities, seem most personally meaningful to us. Those same themes might never even impinge on others' lives, not because they are absent, but because for these others they have no personal meaning.

Without knowing what these themes are, we cannot pinpoint their influence and cannot see how they alter our perceptions of events. Thus, an important task for all of us is to understand the themes that contribute to our stories—such as vulnerability to harm, the feeling that we are entitled to unlimited benefits, the fear of loss of control, the belief that we are unlovable, and so on.[1] If we know, for example, that we have a tendency to feel vulnerable in front of others, we are more likely to recognize that particular feelings of vulnerability stem from our own predisposition to feel vulnerable rather than from an actual injury.

According to the story view, we shape our environment at least as much as the environment shapes us. We do not simply react to whatever a situation throws at us.[2] Rather, through the stories we bring into the world about love and other things, we partially create a world to which we then react. But often we do not recognize or acknowledge this proactive role, which is why we often hear people say, "This just keeps happening to me."

For example, a woman might repeatedly seek out a controlling, abusive partner, then complain that she keeps ending up with horrible losers. She is right, but she may fail to realize the active role she has played in creating this situation. Were Zach and Tammy to split, they would very likely end up in new relationships that resemble war zones. Later, they would be likely to curse their bad luck. Our stories guide not only how we develop in our relationships, but also how the environment we develop helps sustain or extinguish a relationship.

STORIES GUIDE HOW RELATIONSHIPS DEVELOP

Our stories, determined as much by our past as by the people with whom we are presently involved, shape the forms our relationships take. Once we have created a story about someone and about our relationship with that person, we do what the author of any good story does: We try to continue it in a consistent way. No one likes to read a book that blatantly contradicts itself. Similarly, no one likes to be in a love relationship that doesn't make sense in the context of what has happened previously. Therefore, we perceive new events in terms of old stories.

Suppose a wife wants an expensive orthopedic bed. The husband's understanding of her desire might be that she is extremely health-conscious, or that she always wants the latest fad, or that she is spending him into his grave, or that she is a hypochondriac, or any of an infinite number of other things. The husband's understanding of his wife's actions depends a great deal on his love story and the role his wife plays in this story.

Our story thus controls the way we perceive the actions of others, which, in turn, are taken as confirming our story. In fact, the same action or set of actions could confirm any number of stories. Once we have a story, we can interpret almost any events as confirming it, elaborating on the story as we see fit.

Our stories do not necessarily become more accurate over time, but they do become more elaborate. They influence the way we perceive everything our partner does, and how we react in turn. Stories often become self-fulfilling prophecies, as our actions and reactions may lead others to act in ways that we expect them to act, though we fail to realize the extent to which we are shaping their behavior.

Stories not only guide the development of relationships, but also guide which relationships we choose to develop at all. Some people believe that when we choose a lover or spouse from among potential candidates, we begin with a list of rationally chosen attributes and then choose the winner of the contest, based on the scores of each potential partner in terms of those attributes. On the contrary, we often find ourselves choosing the person who would lose any such rational contest. Sometimes we go after a person whom on any rational basis we would reject straightaway. The reason is that in most cases, a story, and not the hard facts, influences us.

This is not to say that rational considerations aren't a factor in our romantic choices. Some of us prefer stories about eternal love; others have stories about money; yet others have stories that feature friendship, control, or punishment. The themes we prefer may be rational or irrational, socially desirable or not. But ultimately, we are attracted to potential partners who enable us to weave joint stories that fit our notion of what we *want* love to be, with less regard to what others might tell us it *should* be. Someone who ensnares us does it not with passion, money, or power, but by offering or appearing to offer a shared love story about money or power or whatever it is we want. We fall in love with a person, but perhaps it is even more accurate to say that we fall in love with our story about a person.

We may or may not marry the person with whom we fall in love. Sometimes we decide to marry the rational choice, whether or not it is the person who conforms best to our story. But when we marry the rational choice—the one that societal or familial dictates suggest as the right choice—we often end up unhappy when we discover that not only do we not love the person, but that we can never grow to love that person. Whether marriage should be about love is one question. But if it is about love, the question of love stories becomes central. If the stories are incompatible, love will be difficult, if not impossible.

Sometimes we have the opposite problem—we know more than one person with whom our stories are compatible in some way.

Emotional involvement with two people simultaneously is not uncommon; it is the theme of many love stories and love songs. One partner is paper-perfect. He or she has all the attributes one imagines oneself to want in a spouse. The other partner can't hold a candle to the first in terms of meeting the qualifications on the mental checklist. Yet one is in love with the second, and loves, but is not in love with, the first. In an age when marriage is supposed to be a love story, people will often go for the second person if forced to make a decision. Consider the case of Maria.

Maria is being courted simultaneously by two men. Sam is everything she's always wanted—intelligent, attractive, successful, considerate, stable. Maria's friends see Sam as a wonderful catch. Kurt looks terrible on paper. He's intelligent, but in a cunning sort of way. He's attractive, but not very successful at work. He blows hot and cold with Maria, paying attention to her for a while, then seeing other women on the weakest of pretexts. Kurt is about as unstable as they come. Yet Maria loves him. She doesn't know why; she only knows it's true. She knows that she should prefer Sam. But it's Kurt she wants. He fits her story of what love is about. Indeed, Maria grew up watching stories of love that were more similar to her relationship with Kurt than to her relationship with Sam. She might like to change her story, but that is easier said than done.

Why are stories hard to change? Consider something psychologists call confirmation bias. People generally seek to confirm, rather than to disconfirm, what they already believe. They will go to great lengths to ignore inconsistent information. Not surprisingly, then, we avoid changing our story about a relationship for as long as we possibly can. Changing an actual story is very uncomfortable. It involves reorganizing a tremendous amount of information, admitting to ourselves that we were wrong, realizing that we are now uncertain about the relationship, and understanding that our new story may also have to be changed. We may come to doubt our feelings, our beliefs, even our trust in a partner. So we tend to keep an old story, even when it is no longer adaptive. Consider an example, the affair.

Why is it often so hard for a partner to get over his or her spouse's affair? Five years ago Jim had a brief affair. Ellen found out from what had been a mutual friend. After an initial denial, Jim admitted to the affair, broke it off, and has not had another since. But for Ellen, the relationship was fundamentally changed. Her actual love story with Jim is altogether different now from what it had been: Jim used to be her Romeo, but now he's turned into Don Juan. Whereas Jim formerly swept Ellen off her feet, Ellen now fears that he could seduce other women this easily as well.

Jim's behavior is basically the same as it was before the affair. Ellen had previously assumed that Jim's attentions could only revolve around her; now she sees him as trying to be attractive to other women, too. How could he show her to be wrong? Ellen is trapped within this Don Juan story. She can't see herself again in the Romeo and Juliet story, but she can't move herself forward to a more workable story line, either. She can't change her story, and it will be difficult for Jim to have any impact in helping her change her story for the better.

It's hard to change other people's stories, because if we attempt to do so, they will often use our attempt to confirm whatever story they already have (e.g., that we try to manipulate them, that we try to control them, that we believe only in our own point of view). Thus, our efforts are likely to backfire, more firmly entrenching the old, undesirable story instead of inaugurating a new one.

Most attempts to change relationships do not work because they attempt to modify cognitions, feelings, or behavior without addressing the story that influences these experiences. But it is hard to address the story when we don't know for sure what it is.

Until the story changes, the relationship cannot change fundamentally. Attempts to adjust relationships virtually never address the story as a whole, but only isolated themes or fragments of it. Even if we manage to change these parts of our love story, any new elements are still likely to be incorporated into the old story.

STORIES CAN CHANGE FOR BETTER OR FOR WORSE

Stories as they play themselves out in relationships change over time, for better or for worse. They become better when we find more and more to like about someone. Curiously, they can change for the worse even if we discover nothing new about a person, because of two psychological phenomena.

The first phenomenon is called the "negative information effect."[3] Negative information is much more powerful than positive information. For example, if we read a letter of recommendation for a job candidate, a single negative statement can devastate the candidate's prospects, no matter how many positive statements there are. One piece of negative information can do more harm than a hundred pieces of positive information can do good. Negative information influences our evaluation more significantly than positive information does. And of course, the negative information may not be negative at all in any objective sense, but only from the standpoint of the story we bring to the information. Thus, we can overvalue negative information, making a person seem worse than he or she really is.

The second phenomenon is called the "fundamental attribution error."[4] We tend to view unfavorable behavior in others as caused by something inherently wrong with them (e.g., a character flaw), whereas we view unfavorable behavior in ourselves as caused by a particular situation. If our partner shouts, it is because she or he is an inherently ill-tempered person; if we shout, it is because we were provoked or are in a bad mood. If our partner does something inconsiderate, it is because she or he is an inconsiderate person; if we do something inconsiderate, it is because we were momentarily distracted. In short, others act badly because they are bad, whereas we act badly because we are temporarily out of sorts or because the situation compels us to do so. Consider the example of Jack and Sandy.

Jack and Sandy seem compatible, if one believes that similarity breeds compatibility. Similarity can sometimes lead to mutual understanding. But not in this situation. Jack and Sandy both have quick tempers. Jack tends to view his flashes of temper as justified by Sandy's frequently unacceptable behavior, whereas he views her temper, ironically, as a basic character flaw. Unfortunately, Sandy's view of the situation is the mirror image of Jack's. The result is a pattern of constantly escalating conflict. Their relationship would be significantly improved if they applied to themselves the same standards they each apply to the other, or to each other the same standards they apply to themselves.

Over time, both the negative information effect and the fundamental attribution error will often render the stories played out in relationships less and less favorable toward our partner. Because it is so difficult to change a story consciously, the change is likely to be not only gradual but preconscious: We don't even realize that it is happening. Over time, what began as a pleasant story has become an unpleasant one. Eventually, the preconscious story becomes conscious; this is the moment when we realize that we are unhappy. The story is no longer what we want it to be; had it been like this in the first place, we might not have entered the partnership. Having reached this point, whatever our partner does will only fit into a less favorable, rather than a more favorable, understanding of the situation.

Stories can change positively, however, if we are aware of the themes of our own stories and of how we process information. If we understand how the negative information effect and the fundamental attribution error can mislead us, and if we realize that not only do relationships affect stories but also that stories affect relationships, we can take a step toward improving our relationship by recognizing that the flaws we are attributing to our partner are really in our own processing of information about the partner, not in the partner him- or herself.

WHY CONVENTIONAL ATTEMPTS TO CHANGE RELATIONSHIPS OFTEN FAIL

Why do attempts to change relationships, whether through the couple's own efforts or through marital therapy, fail so often? They fail because they ignore the stories that guide each person's view of and approach to the relationship.

Almost all of us have been involved in one or more relationships that didn't work. Often, the decision to break up is not mutual, and the person who is left behind seeks to know why, from the other person's point of view, the relationship fell apart. The person who has broken matters off sometimes feels as though he or she is contriving reasons to provide an answer to why the relationship failed, not only for the partner, but also for himself. The person who was left behind may also feel this way. They are both correct. What they believe to be causes of the dissolution of the relationship are actually effects. We *create* reasons for the breakup, just as we once created reasons for getting together. The reasons are apparent rather than real. They may be that the partner was too demanding, or communication was not all it could be, or the relationship was not progressing, or any of a multitude of other reasons. In essence, we believe we are thinking in the rational mode when in fact the thinking that is driving us is in the narrative, intuitive mode.

These "reasons" are rarely the "causes" of the breakdown. We make up these reasons in order to justify to ourselves and to others what we have done. The real reason for the breakup is that we no longer like the way our story is playing itself out. Stories are hard to change, but they do change over time. What started out as a story we liked has become one we don't.

The behavior that we tolerated before, we now no longer tolerate, not because the behavior has changed, but because it is now part of a bad story playing itself out. The very things we used to like about the person we no longer like, because they now remind us of the bad story. To change the relationship, we need to understand the story and address it. And we also need to understand our own and our partner's ideal story, which is probably what got us together in the first place. Consider Gary and Carla.

When he was trying to recover from an alcohol problem, Gary was enchanted by Carla's nurturance. She couldn't do enough for him; she was always there when he needed her, and she was selfless in her devotion to Gary's recovery. Carla hasn't changed, but Gary's attitude toward her has. Gary now feels smothered by Carla. He needs space and feels that Carla won't give it to him. He knows she means well, but she is now part of his story of recovery from addiction, a story that he would like, by and large, to forget. The very behaviors he once admired so much are now a source of smoldering resentment. What was once Gary's ideal story no longer exists.

UNDERSTANDING IDEAL STORIES

To understand our partner's feelings about us, we need to understand our partner's story about ideal relationships. Often, because the story is preconscious, our partner is not entirely aware of it, any more than we are aware of our own ideal story.

The particular stories we develop are, I believe, a composite of the attributes of persons in our past whom we have wanted in some way but have been unable to have. We lose a parent; we are rejected as kids by other children who make fun of us; we have teenage heartthrobs and heartbreaks. Each time we lose someone, we internalize those attributes that appealed to us, and eventually build up, usually unconsciously, a composite of the attributes of which we have been deprived in the past.

Our research at Yale has shown that people have ideals for love relationships, and that these ideals are every bit as important as the actual relationship itself.[5] The ideals control not only how we form our actual story, but also how happy we are with it. Furthermore, we feel emotion when we sense a match between an actual or potential story and our ideal one. The cognition of a match thus generates positive emotions, like happiness and contentment. Negative emotions, like sadness, anger, and frustration, may come about when we expect or hope for a match and it doesn't occur.[6] Sometimes we try to force a match. When we meet someone, we determine how close the person is to our ideal. If he or she doesn't match at all, then we can simply dismiss the person. If the person is close, however, then we are likely to try to remake that person into our ideal. In other words, we will interpret the actions of the other in order to fit our rosiest imaginings. We want our ideal story to come true.

Many of us have been in relationships in which we have felt that either our own or the other's involvement in the relationship is based on self-perpetuating illusions about ideals that do not match realities. Ultimately, the illusion may come crashing down if the actions and statements of the partner eventually can no longer support increasingly strained efforts to maintain a plausible fiction. Consider the example of Liz and Larry.

Liz was always attracted to the strong and silent type. When she met Larry, she used to spend hours trying to puzzle out what he was thinking. Larry was not big on giving compliments, but when he did give one, Liz was on cloud nine. The relationship was an exciting one, because for Liz, the ideal story was one in which most of what happened was inside—beneath the surface. Now Larry and Liz have been married for three years, and Liz has come to a terrible realization. Underneath Larry's silence is a void. He's not like an artichoke, with a hidden core, but like an onion instead: When you peel away the layers of Larry's reticence, you find nothing left underneath. Larry was silent for all those years because he had nothing to say. Liz now realizes that she imagined Larry to be something he was not. The trouble is, it's too late to do anything without radically changing both their lives.

Some potential partners immediately fit into our ideal stories, leading to feelings of infatuation, whereas other potential partners do not. If love develops slowly out of friendship, we may sense a slow change in our ideal story to fit our current relationship. The new ideal story does not necessarily replace the old one, but may exist side by side with it. In this event, there is always the possibility that we may later meet someone who is more compatible with our original ideal. If that story has retained its hold on us, we may find ourselves wanting either to switch relationships or to be involved in both simultaneously.

Of course, ideals may or may not change, but relationships always do. As they change, they can move partners toward more or less satisfaction. Oftentimes, many people who start off with stories that are less realistic or at least less easy to sustain in long-term relationships, such as fantasy or mystery stories, find that the stories begin to unravel as responsibilities increase—those of maintaining a household, bringing up children, and paying taxes. These elements may fit well into a business story, for example, but much less well into a fairy-tale story—a story in which a prince seeks his princess, or vice versa. As a result, people with certain stories that cannot be easily sustained may find themselves becoming disillusioned more rapidly than people who have more viable stories.

Sometimes disillusionment leads to a change of partner. Essentially, the ideal story stays constant, and the person tries to change the actual story. For example, a man or a woman with an art story—someone who seeks a work of art in a partner—may start to feel disappointment as his or her partner ages. Sometimes men in their middle age turn to younger women, making it easier for the men to sustain an art story as a love relationship, or, for that matter, a government story because of the greater power the older man is likely to have or feel he has in the relationship with the younger woman. Other stories, too, can lead a man to turn to a younger woman, or a woman to turn to a different sort of man—for example, a woman may find a more successful business partner in a more established man. Stories are an important element in changing partners, but so is the cultural context in which stories are embedded.

STORIES WE'RE SUPPOSED TO TELL: THE CULTURAL MATRIX

The stories we tell are unique prototypes—appropriate for our particular time and place.[7] They are embedded in a cultural matrix.[8] Cultures approve of certain stories and disapprove of others. For example, in the United States today, marriage is supposed to be a story of true love. Historically, this is a rarity. Contemporary Americans consider it gauche to marry simply for money or status, whereas such a story would have been considered acceptable and even desirable throughout most of history.

Thus, although we create our own stories, we do so within the context of our cultural mores. We are under continual, although usually subtle, pressure to create only those stories that are culturally acceptable. People may be executed in one time or place for a story—about adultery, for example—that in another time or place would scarcely raise an eyebrow.

Moreover, our love story is only one of many stories we create.[9] We create stories about other topics as well, such as our jobs and family. We think of how we prefer to envision ourselves at work and with other members of our family. These stories are sometimes complementary, but may also compete with our love stories. Thus, some people have difficulty making their love and work stories mesh, with the result that they are in a constant state of tension. Some people actually prefer to combine the various stories of their lives into a single story, while others keep them more separate. For example, someone who likes to combine stories might prefer to be in a close relationship with a colleague at work, whereas someone who likes to keep stories separate would never think of entering such a relationship. But most people strive for cognitive consistency—a neat fitting of the stories with one another. To understand our love story fully, we need to appreciate how it fits into the total context of our lives. Consider the case of Ben and Lisa.

Ben loves Lisa, but unbeknownst to Lisa, he will never marry her. Even Ben doesn't like to admit it to himself. Ben is an assistant vice president of a large bank. Everyone knows that to work your way up the ladder at the bank, you can marry only a certain type of partner. She's got to be someone who makes you look good at the bank's social functions. She has to look right, speak right, and know how to entertain. She has to be from the right kind of background. No one talks about it, because life in the modern age isn't supposed to be this way. But it is that way at the bank. Lisa's great, but marrying her would be a ticket to oblivion for Ben's career. So he waits, knowing he will have to move on to a different relationship, but not having it in his heart to do so. Lisa simply doesn't fit the story Ben needs to succeed at work. If Lisa had understood Ben's story, she never would have entered into the relationship.

Understanding our own stories and those of our partner is critically important in the formation of a relationship as well as in changing it. This understanding helps us enormously in finding the right partner from the outset. Let's consider now just what the stories are, and how they operate in the context of our daily lives.

⚋ 11 LOVE STORIES

Love Stories can be grouped in a variety of ways. Just as there is no final set of stories, so is there no final grouping. As new stories are created, groupings can change. The grouping used here focuses on internal characteristics of the stories. It is an a priori grouping, rather than one revealed through statistical analysis. It may help you understand better the demands different kinds of stories place on relationships. There are five major kinds of stories.

Asymmetrical stories are founded on the idea that asymmetry (or complementary behavior) between partners should be the basis of an intimate relationship. In a teacher-student story, one individual provides structure and information, the other individual receives it. In the sacrifice story, one individual willingly makes concessions, the other receives the concessions and is the beneficiary of them. In a government story, one individual holds power over another individual. (In an alternative form of government story, which is a coordination story, as described below, the individuals share power.) In a police story, one individual conducts surveillance on and often provides structure for the other. In a pornography story, one individual debases another. In a horror story, one individual is a tormentor, the other the victim of the debasement. In these stories, which individual is in which role can change over time or even across situations. But the relationship tends to be asymmetrical at any given time, regardless of who is in which role.

Object stories are stories in which the partner or the relationship largely seem to be means toward some end outside or beyond the relationship. Object stories are of two principal kinds. In one kind, a person is the object. In all of these stories, the partner is valued not for himself or herself but for the role the partner plays. In a science-fiction story, the oddness or weirdness of the partner is valued. In a collection story, the partner is valued as a part of a larger collection. In an art story, the physical appearance of the partner is valued. In the second kind of object story, the relationship is the object. In this kind of story, the relationship is a means to achieving or finding something that's important that is essentially outside the relationship. In a house and home story, the relationship is a means to achieving a stable and usually beautiful house and home environment. In a recovery story, the relationship is a means to recover from a trauma of some kind. In a religion story, the relationship serves to help one or both partners come close to God, or else the relationship itself becomes a kind of religion. In a game story, the partners want to win, in general, and the relationship provides a game to win.

Coordination stories are based on the notion of partners working together to create or do or maintain something. In a travel story, love is a journey, and the partners work together to choose and arrive at their mutual destination. In a sewing and knitting story, relationships are sewed or knitted by the two partners working together. In a garden story, the partners nurture the relationship the way gardeners would. In a business story, the partners create a business involving a specified division of labor. In an addiction story, one partner cannot exist without the other, at least within the context of a dependency that seems essential to the partner's life.

Narrative stories draw on the idea that there is some sort of text, which exists outside the relationship, and which is prescriptive of the way in which the relationship should go. In a fantasy story, the text focuses on the fairy story involving a prince and a princess, or a knight and a princess. In a history story, the text focuses on the past as it applies to and leads into the present. In a science story, the text consists of how relationships can be analyzed according to preexisting scientific principles and formulas. In a cookbook story, the text consists of a recipe that, if followed, will lead to success in the relationship.

Genre stories emphasize the mode or way of being in the relationship, rather than the aims of the relationship or any underlying principles behind the relationship. In a war story, what's important are the battles and the war behind them, rather than any particular goals of the battles or the war. In a theater story, what's important is that one partner is constantly acting a role, whatever the role may happen to be (and indeed, the role may change over time). In a humor story, what's important is that the relationship is lighthearted and is never allowed to become too serious. And in a mystery story, what's important is that one partner constantly uncovers information about the other, whatever that information may be, or whatever its importance may be.

In this part of the book, I consider each of the love stories individually, describing the story briefly, presenting statements from an inventory we use to assess people's love stories, giving examples of each love story, describing modes of thought and behavior characteristic of each love story, explaining the roles people play in each story, and discussing advantages and disadvantages of each story.

The inventory statements supplied with each story are used to get a sense of people's stories of love. In our studies, people rate themselves for each statement, usually on a scale of 1 to 9, where 1 means that a given statement does not characterize them at all, and 9 means that it characterizes them extremely well. (Sometimes we use other scales, such as 1 to 7.) Scores are averaged for the multiple statements pertaining to each story, giving us a profile of the extent to which each story applies to each person. In general, averaged scores of 7 to 9 are high, indicating an attraction to a story, and scores of 1 to 3 are low, indicating little or no interest in the story at all. Moderate scores of 4 to 6 indicate some interest, but probably not enough to generate or keep a romantic interest.

Because the description of each story includes the inventory items we use in our research, you might wish to respond to these items yourself, rating on the 1 to 9 scale the extent to which each item characterizes you in your close relationships. You can then evaluate your own profile of preferred stories, assessing the extent to which each story characterizes you in your relationships. You will notice that some of the items seem to say almost the same thing as do other items, only with slightly different wording. There are three reasons for such overlap. First, longer tests tend to give more reliable (replicable) measurements. Second, even slight changes in wording of questionnaires can influence responses, sometimes even drastically. Third, people for whom a story is more representative are more likely to give the same high ratings across variations in wording than are people for whom that story is less representative.

ASYMMETRICAL STORIES

Asymmetrical stories, as mentioned earlier, are based on the notion that an asymmetry between partners should be a fundamental basis of a close relationship. Six kinds of asymmetrical stories are: the teacher-student story, the sacrifice story, the government story, the police story, the pornography story, and the horror story.

⌐ THE TEACHER-STUDENT STORY

The teacher-student story is one of inherent asymmetry. In this story, one partner enjoys the role of teacher, and the other partner takes pleasure in the role of learner. In some cases, the partners may switch their roles in different areas—for example, one person may be the teacher when it comes to the relationship, while the other takes the lead in dealing with the outside world. Commonly, though, one individual is older chronologically or more mature professionally than the other, and it is not rare for these relationships actually to be between teachers and students, or supervisors and supervisees. In these cases, there are differences in power and usually in experience built into the relationship, and this most often results in the older or more senior person taking on the role of teacher. In any case, what is important in the story of this and other kinds of relationships is the attribution—that is, how the people involved define their roles.[1] The asymmetry is in the attribution, not in any actual fact. Indeed, the person labeled as the teacher may have little or nothing to teach, or what he or she teaches may be utter nonsense.

Diagnosing the Teacher-Student Story

TEACHER

1   I find myself in the role of a teacher in my close relationships.
2   I tend to find myself teaching my partners in close relationships a lot about life.
3   I sometimes feel as though the people with whom I am in relationships are like my students.
4   I like the fact that the people with whom I am in relationships have a lot to learn from me.

STUDENT

1   I find myself in the role of a student in my close relationships.
2   I tend to find myself learning quite a bit from my partners in close relationships.
3   I sometimes feel as though the people with whom I am in relationships are like teachers to me.
4   I like the fact that the people with whom I am in relationships have a lot to teach me.

David and Jessica

It is almost one in the morning, but David and Jessica are still talking to each other on the phone. Actually, to be more precise, David is talking and Jessica is listening. Earlier this evening they both attended their company's sales awards ceremony, and David is explaining to his girlfriend why he hated it so much. He tells her of the elitism that these ceremonies represent—how the company shuts out everyone who does not measure up to its arbitrary standards of excellence.

The company pretends to be a proponent of all people—the smart, the dumb, the beautiful, the ugly—so long as they sell. But it hypocritically rejects all those who do not fit into its mold. Under the veil of freedom and individuality, the company is nothing more than a politically correct eugenics movement. David goes on to criticize the whole notion of sales success that the evening's festivities embodied, arguing that the idea of sales achievement as success is nothing more than an illusory carrot that is dangled in front of our eyes, blinding us to the whole world that we pass by while chasing after it.

Since David and Jessica started going out six months ago, there have been many evenings like this one, with David philosophizing about life and Jessica soaking it all in. Although one might suspect that Jessica would regard David's almost professorial stance as condescending, Jessica does not see it this way; in fact, she enjoys listening to David's intelligent and novel perspective on the world, and believes that she has learned quite a bit since the start of their relationship. Moreover, not only does she feel that she has learned many things about life in general, but she also thinks that she has gained a considerably greater knowledge of herself.

Indeed, David's discussions are not merely impersonal lectures that he could just as easily give to a classroom of pupils; for the most part, they are aimed specifically at Jessica. For example, before meeting David, Jessica always wanted to make senior sales manager. She had imagined that such a job would provide her with both a comfortable living and an opportunity to help people. David has repeatedly described to her the other aspects of being a senior manager of any kind. He has told her of the hypocrisy, greed, and selfishness that he has seen infiltrate into the top ranks of the company; he has mentioned how difficult it is to get higher up in the company without manipulating people along the way. Jessica realizes that much, although perhaps not all, of what David says is true.

Needless to say, David holds an extreme, controversial position; nevertheless, his words have had a major effect on Jessica's plans. She now believes that she would rather eventually find some other job that will not require her to sacrifice her personal integrity.

For all the relationship's strengths, Jessica believes that there are some problems with it. For one, David's philosophizing sometimes takes time away from other valuable things that they could be doing together. Often, David is so busy telling her about life that they seem rarely to have the time to live that life. But, she realizes, that's David.

Jenny and Jonathan

Jenny sits with her best friend, Paula, on a bench in the park; she is telling Paula about the problems she is having with her boyfriend, Jonathan. Jenny has been seeing Jonathan for almost six months, and she is becoming very distressed by the way he listens to her every word as if she were preaching some sort of divine truth. To illustrate, she tells Paula about an incident that took place last night.

They were watching a movie at her apartment, and Jonathan started asking Jenny what she thought the metaphorical significance of the movie was. At first she gave him an honest assessment, and with every line she uttered, he nodded in agreement. She became annoyed with his indefatigable acquiescence to her views and started to wish that he would argue with her every once in a while, that he would start voicing some opinions of his own. In an effort to get him to do so, Jenny began turning her actual assessment of the movie into a completely random litany of irrelevant comments. Incredibly, although he occasionally expressed some confusion, he continued to agree with her views.

In the early stages of her relationship with Jonathan, Jenny actually appreciated the way he attentively listened to and approved of what she said. She thought she had found a soul mate—someone who finally agreed with her unusual outlook on the world. They spent many hours talking about her various beliefs and opinions, and neither of them seemed to tire of it. When they would engage in a discussion with a group of friends, or with some people at a party, Jonathan would always come to her defense if one of her views was disputed. In many ways they had assumed the roles of teacher and prize student; in fact, one of Jenny's friends likened it to the relationship that existed between Socrates and Plato, with Jenny imparting her philosophical wisdom to the eager ears of Jonathan. However, as time went on, it became apparent to Jenny that Jonathan, unlike Plato, was not coming up with any theories of his own;

he was nothing more than her echo, mimicking her words and actions whenever they were together. At times, she almost began to feel suffocated by his presence.

Jenny tells Paula that she somehow feels responsible for how her relationship with Jonathan turned out. She believes that had she not been so eager to tell him every aspect of her philosophical outlook on the world, he would not have been as likely to assume his somewhat subservient role as her student. Moreover, she realizes that the excitement she showed when he agreed with her most likely perpetuated his acquiescence even more. Hence, although she has become concerned about Jonathan's parroting behavior, she recognizes that it is partly her fault.

Modes of Thought and Behavior

In a teacher-student relationship, an asymmetry is created by one partner taking on the role of teacher and other assuming the role of student. People in this kind of relationship have trouble achieving parity or any kind of symmetry. Either one person will be the teacher in every area of the relationship, or else roles will alternate in different areas. In either case, though, there is an inherent asymmetry in the couple's interactions.

These relationships sometimes derive from actual roles at school or at work. Such relationships are extremely difficult to develop, not only because of the inherent power differential of teacher and student or boss and employee, but because they are generally frowned upon both in school and in the workplace. The "teacher" is often seen as taking advantage of his or her power, whereas the "student" is seen as taking advantage of the personal relationship to advance him-or herself professionally.

People in such relationships will often go to great lengths to conceal the relationship, and hence it is surprising how almost uniformly unsuccessful they are in doing so. Couples can leak so many different kinds of signals indicating they are involved that all but the most assiduous and careful will usually fail at some point in their attempt at concealment. When the relationship then comes out into the open, coworkers or other students feel betrayed, not only by the relationship, but by its concealment. Indeed, the concealment supports people's natural hypothesis that the couple truly did have something to hide.

The situation is complicated even further when the relationship is in addition to a primary relationship for one or both partners. Although extramarital relationships are not uncommon, they impose a particular burden when they occur in a workplace, because they are even more likely to be interpreted as being about power and advancement rather than about love. People with this story may feel divided loyalties, moreover, and find themselves in very uncomfortable roles as they try to figure out how to handle a relationship that is increasingly becoming untenable. Clearly, couples in such relationships, if they decide to continue them, would be best off putting themselves in different working groups so as to reduce, if not to eliminate altogether, the frictions that arise when two people in a work group are also in a close personal relationship.

Complementary Roles: Teacher and Student

The complementary roles in the relationship are those of teacher and student, either in all matters or within only one area. If the partners share roles of teacher and student, they can learn a lot from each other and potentially maintain a balance of power in the relationship. If one partner is always the teacher and the other always the learner, there is bound to be an imbalance of power in the relationship in favor of the teacher.

Advantages and Disadvantages

The greatest potential advantage of teacher-student relationships is that they fulfill the couple's goals: One enjoys being a teacher, and the other finds learning enjoyable. Or they both enjoy both roles, but in different areas.

But these relationships carry with them a number of inherent disadvantages. If the couple is in the same work group, they typically cause problems for coworkers, and eventually for themselves. If they are not in such a group, the inherent imbalance in power may, for some people, become uncomfortable. Moreover, the student in the relationship may eventually no longer feel like continuing in the student role, at which point the teacher-student story may exhaust itself, at least for this partner, although possibly not for the other.

☞ THE SACRIFICE STORY

All close relationships involve occasional sacrifices made by one partner for the other. In a sacrifice story, however, one individual repeatedly and consistently makes sacrifices, or views him or herself as making sacrifices, for the other. The individual shows what John Lee has called agapic love.[1] The giving of self is part of what drives the love, and the individual is not really happy unless he or she is primarily in the role of giver rather than taker.

Love of God may have this character, whereby sacrifice can be part of the relationship a person sees him-or herself as having with God or some other deity. The individual may feel loved, in return, by the deity, but must make sacrifices in favor of the deity. At the same time, there may have been, or continue to be, sacrifices on the part of the deity, as in the case of the story of Jesus. Sacrifice relationships can and frequently do also involve children, parents, or other relations.

Diagnosing the Sacrifice Story

1 I often enjoy making sacrifices for the sake of my partner.
2 I believe that being prepared to make sacrifices for your partner is the sign of true love.
3 I would not hesitate to sacrifice for the sake of my partner.
4 I often give up something that I would like to do for the sake of my partner. Yet, knowing that my partner is happy makes me happy.
5 I believe a close relationship is not only about love, but also about sacrifices for love.

6   I believe sacrifice is a key part of true love.

7   I frequently make sacrifices for the good of my partner.

8   I often compromise my own comforts in order to satisfy my partner's needs.

Wanda and Derek

Wanda grew up in a home with a very dominant father and a very submissive mother. There was no doubt about who was in charge. In the 1950s, that was the way things were supposed to be, or at least that's what both of Wanda's parents thought. Looking back, Wanda is thoroughly disgusted with the subservience her mother showed toward her father at every turn.

Wanda is determined to do things differently. She has a promising career ahead of her in management, and she is determined to climb the corporate ladder just as high as she can. Derek, her boyfriend, is wonderfully supportive of her plans. Wanda could hardly be happier. She's got a great career and a caring lover. What more could she want?

Actually, there is one other thing she could want. Derek is just finishing medical school, and is applying for internships. The problem is that the internships available in the local area are not prestigious ones. Both Derek and the people around him see him as a very promising doctor—certainly someone who can do better than to take one of the local internships. But a good internship would mean a move.

Derek points out to Wanda that there are good business opportunities in all of the cities that he is considering for good internships. With what Derek sees as Wanda's greater potential flexibility with respect to location, he is hoping that she will be willing to move for him. Of course, he points out, they could separate for the years of the internship; but Derek also points that they both know how hard it is for couples to stay together even when they are living in the same city. Separation might be the kiss of death—something that he certainly doesn't want to experience, and that he is sure Wanda doesn't want to experience either.

Wanda is reluctant to move, but feels she has no choice. She really wants Derek to have the promising career that awaits him, and after all, he is correct in saying that there will be business opportunities in any of the cities they might go to. She wants to succeed, and it's clear Derek wants her to succeed, too—not like the story of her mother and father, where her mother was always expected to make mindless sacrifices for her father. No, not like that story at all. Wanda sees she will have to make the move, but she feels like something is wrong. She's just not sure what the something is.

Vince and Eva

Vince is thirty-two and frustrated. He wants to marry Eva, but he isn't sure she wants to marry him. They have been dating for five years, and she has given him what amounts to an ultimatum— pretty amazing, given that he has proposed to her at least a dozen times.

Of course, the ultimatum isn't about marriage. It's about Vince's living arrangements, and about where he and Eva would live and what their life would be like if they were to marry.

Vince lives with his mother, who is eighty-eight. She is in failing health, as she has been for the past ten years. Her friends, not to mention her doctors, are astonished that she is still alive. But she seems determined to confound friends, doctors—really, anyone who bets against her survival.

Vince can understand Eva's reluctance to move into the house with him and his mother. It isn't exactly his ideal for a couple of newlyweds, either. Vince just doesn't believe he can leave his mother alone, and he doesn't want to put her in a nursing home. Caring for his mother is no mean feat—it probably consumes three or four hours a day, which, on top of his work life, doesn't always leave him much time for Eva. He has pointed out to Eva that his mother won't live forever. But his pointing that out just leads to the same old fight every time. She responds—correctly—that he has been singing the same tune for the past five years, and his mother is still around. She is happy that his mother is still alive, but she just cannot move into the house with Vince and his mother, especially given that Vince is spending so many hours a day caring for his mother.

Vince realizes that he is likely to lose Eva, but he just doesn't see any alternative. The thought of losing her depresses him. Aside from their arguments over the potential living arrangements, their relationship has been wonderful, and Eva has been very caring toward him, and even toward his mother. She just doesn't want to live with his mother. He has to care for his mother; there's just no alternative. And if Eva can't see that, then he will just have to find someone who can.

Modes of Thought and Behavior

People with a sacrifice story typically give without much hope or even expectation of equal return. Or they may feel that the return they get is from their giving. For example, they experience more joy in giving than in receiving a birthday present or other present. They may also feel that they receive a lot in return, although the return may be in a form that is not tangible, or obvious to others.

A key feature of the sacrifice story is that those who hold it often see it as a necessity rather than as a choice. At some level, Wanda has a choice of whether or not she should move with Derek. But she is not experiencing her situation as a choice. She really believes that moving is what she *should* do, and that if she does not move, it is because something is wrong with her. Although one could argue in favor of or against her moving, the key mode of thinking here is the absence of a perceived choice, despite the existence of one. In this sense, she is repeating her mother's pattern. Her mother, too, probably saw herself as doing what she had to do.

Similarly, Vince could view himself as having a choice, but he doesn't. He has not really investigated all possible options regarding his mother's living arrangement, and probably won't, given the amount of time that has passed without his conducting such an investigation. He feels locked into his decision—as though what he is doing is right, and anything else he might do would simply be wrong. He would view himself as less of a person were he to make any other choice, the same way Wanda views her situation.

People with a sacrifice story can be seen as overly giving, which in a sense they are; but it needs to be remembered that giving is their story. Although they may complain about their giving, or even throw it in the face of the person to whom they give, they have a story about love that will always place them in the role of the giver, pretty much without regard to the circumstances. And if the circumstances do not require them to give, they will try to construct situations that will enable them to be givers. In the extreme, others may see them as having a "martyr complex," because they may seem to enjoy the role of giving without receiving equally in return.

Complementary Roles: Sacrificer and Beneficiary

The two complementary roles in a sacrifice story are of the sacrificer and the beneficiary—that is, the one who sacrifices and the one who receives the sacrifices. Most commonly, one individual occupies the sacrificer role all of the time, and the other individual always takes the role of beneficiary. Less commonly, when both people are sacrificers, it will typically be in different domains. For example, a husband might sacrifice in the professional domain for his wife, but she might sacrifice for her husband in the financial domain. The wife may let the husband spend as much as he wants of the money achieved as a result of her professional gain.

Advantages and Disadvantages

The sacrifice story can lead to happy relationships when both partners are content in the roles they are playing, particularly when both make sacrifices (typically, in different domains). It is likely to lead to friction when the partners are playing roles they don't consciously want to play, but that unconsciously they feel compelled to play anyway.

Research suggests that relationships of all kinds tend to be happiest when they are roughly equitable,[2] although in successful close relationships, people generally do not view the relationship as a simple tit-for-tat affair, where careful accounts are kept of what each individual gives and receives.[3] The greatest risk factor in a sacrifice story is probably that the give-and-take in the relationship will become so out of balance that one or both partners will start to feel uncomfortable.

What makes the situation even more difficult is that the story of one or both partners tends to perpetuate this imbalance. Thus, an individual may resent always being the giver, but continue doing it anyway, not necessarily because the other partner requests it, but because it is the individual's story of love. Similarly, the receiver may feel uncomfortable being so often on the receiving end, but be unable to change the behavior of the sacrificer, even when the giver is resentful of so often making sacrifices.

When a point of discomfort is reached, some restoration of balance is necessary, but first, both individuals must recognize the story that is driving the sacrificing behavior.

⌒ THE GOVERNMENT STORY

Government stories can take a number of different forms, but all of these forms have in common one theme—concern with distribution of power. The forms differ in large part as a function of how power is distributed between the two people in the relationship.

In an autocratic relationship, one partner takes on virtually all the power. He or she makes the decisions, and then decides how the decisions are to be implemented, who will implement them, and where and when they will be implemented. In these relationships, one person essentially becomes the governor, or autocrat, and the other becomes the governed, or subject.

Relationships can become autocratic for any of a number of reasons. One reason is religious: Some religions vest almost all of the power in a relationship with the man. An example of this was seen when the Taliban militia, fundamentalist Muslims, took over major portions of Afghanistan in 1996 and immediately dismissed women from jobs and girls from schools. They left no question as to who was supposed to be the boss in that society.

A second way in which a relationship can become autocratic is as a result of one partner's very high need for power.[1] Some people just have high power needs and use the intimate relationship as a means to express them. Someone with a strong desire for power whose needs are suppressed at work can become particularly tyrannical in the home, as the individual uses the home as a way of compensating for the frustration he or she is experiencing at work.

A third route to autocracy is mutual consent. The couple feels more comfortable with one person making the decisions and taking responsibility for enacting them. Usually, one individual in such a relationship is very submissive, and prefers to have as little responsibility for decisions as possible.

Government relationships can also be democratic and egalitarian, in which case power is more or less equally shared between the partners. In a democratic relationship, some decisions may be made primarily or even exclusively by one or the other partner. The principle is equal distribution of power on average, not necessarily equal voice in every single decision that is made. When the government story unfolds in this way, it functions more like a coordination story (see page 135).

A fourth power-sharing arrangement, which is probably less common than the autocratic or democratic ones, is anarchic. No one takes responsibility for solving problems or making decisions; each partner is usually hoping that the other will be the responsible one. Such relationships tend to be disorganized, and also to result in a disorganized lifestyle. Such couples are at risk for sliding down the socioeconomic scale, because no one is making sure that what needs to get done is in fact getting done.

Diagnosing the Government Story

AUTOCRATIC (GOVERNOR)

1   It is important to me to be the sole person in control of important decisions in my close relationships.
2   I believe relationships are fundamentally about who is controlling whom, and I certainly don't want to be the one who is being controlled.
3   I think it is important to let my partner know from the outset that I will be in charge.
4   I like to be the sole person in charge of important decisions, because otherwise there will be anarchy.

AUTOCRATIC (GOVERNED)

1   I believe relationships are like governments; one person should be responsible for all the decisions, and I would rather let my partner be that person.
2   I don't mind if my partner makes most of the decisions because I think it is better to have one person in charge.
3   I think it is important for one person to be responsible for important decisions in a relationship, and I would rather let my partner be the responsible one.
4   I think it is actually more efficient if only one person takes control of the important decisions in a relationship, and I don't mind if that person is not me.

DEMOCRATIC

1   I believe relationships are all about sharing of power, just as governments are.
2   I believe, contrary to what many people believe, that the issues of love and power can be resolved, provided partners are willing to share both love and power.
3   I believe it is important for partners in any close relationship to learn from the outset how to make important decisions together.
4   It is important that my partner and I share in the process of decision making.
5   I believe the only way that partners can form a harmonious relationship together is if they share in the power.
6   I believe the only way to maintain equality for partners in a relationship is to share power.
7   I believe relationships are all about learning to share everything, including power.
8   I believe sharing of power is essential to a close relationship, just as sharing of power is essential to a government.

Jerry and Kristen

Jerry and Kristen have been going out for almost two years, and for the most part everything appears to be just fine. Indeed, everyone who knows them is convinced that someday they will get married. Several of Jerry's friends, however, are becoming concerned that Kristen is controlling Jerry. He no longer hangs out with them as often as he used to, and whenever he does, Kristen always seems to be there with him, ready to take him away at a moment's notice.

The other night, Jerry and his friends were in the middle of watching the NCAA championship basketball game—a game they had been talking about all week long—when Kristen suddenly appeared at the door. There were only six minutes left in the game and the score was tied, so the last thing anyone wanted was an interruption. Kristen walked right up to Jerry and told him that she needed to talk to him. He asked politely if it could wait until the end of the game, but she told him that it was important to her that he come outside and talk to her right away. Jerry's friends continued to stare at the television, although they were too interested in what was going on in the background to pay much attention to the game. As Jerry got up and left the room with Kristen, they all turned to one another and started shaking their heads in disbelief. Jerry did not return until after the game had already ended; when he did, he acted as though there was nothing unusual about what had just happened.

Up until this episode, Jerry's friends were not sure whether they should confront Jerry about his relationship with Kristen. After all, even though they regarded his situation as less than optimal, Jerry never indicated to them that he felt there was any problem. However, the basketball episode seemed sufficiently peculiar to warrant a discussion. As a result, Jerry's friends have decided that it would be best to talk to him about their concerns; perhaps Jerry really is troubled by his relationship with Kristen, but is just too embarrassed to approach anyone about it.

In response to the concerns of his friends, Jerry remarks, to everyone's surprise, that he is well aware of the control that Kristen exerts over him, but insists that it does not bother him. Jerry tells his friends that he appreciates their concern for him, but assures them that he has no problem with the fact that Kristen makes most of the decisions in their relationship. He tells them he does not want to bother making these kind of mundane and trivial decisions: He has more important things to do. He is aware that many people would regard his situation as an unfortunate one, but he feels very comfortable with it. His friends remain confused, but they see that Jerry is happy with his relationship, and realize that this is the most important thing of all.

Nancy and Ted

Nancy and her husband, Ted, both feel that power is an integral part of their relationship. However, they recognize that if they do not share this power, they will run the risk of having a tyrannical relationship. As a result, they believe that Ted should be in charge of certain matters and Nancy should be in charge of others. In areas over which Ted is in charge, Nancy is allowed to make suggestions, but it is Ted who makes the final decision. Likewise, in areas over which Nancy is in charge, Ted is allowed to make suggestions, but it is Nancy who makes the final decisions. Understandably, problems occasionally arise over certain decisions. In fact, Ted and Nancy recently had a dispute regarding their fifteen-year-old daughter, Julia.

Sixteen-year-old Ken came over one night to pick up Julia before going to a movie. Ted thought that Ken seemed reckless, and also felt that Ken's attire—ripped jeans and a ratty T-shirt—was completely unacceptable. After Julia returned from the movie, Ted told her that she would no longer be allowed to go out with Ken. Julia thought that this was absolutely absurd; she went to her mother and asked her to reason with Ted. Nancy agreed with Julia's assessment of the situation and tried to convince Ted that his decision was too rash. Nancy argued that although Ken's attire might have been inappropriate for a fancy dinner, it was in fact acceptable for a movie.

Regarding Ken's recklessness, Nancy thought Ted should not judge Ken after just one meeting. Ted listened to his wife but was not swayed by her arguments, and he maintained that his decision was final. Nancy could only shake her head. After all, Ted is in charge of supervising Julia's social life. Nancy is allowed her input, but it is Ted who has the final word.

A couple of days later, Julia confronted her father about his decision, telling him that it was unfair for him to decide arbitrarily that she would no longer be allowed to go out with Ken. In a calm yet direct voice, Ted told her that it was intolerable for her to go out with someone as slovenly and reckless as Ken was. Julia asked her mother for some defense, but Nancy simply told her that Ted's decision was final. Julia stormed up to her room, angrily yelling at her mother for her obsequious behavior. Julia's words had an almost instantaneous effect on her mother. Nancy turned to Ted and, in a serious tone, told him to recall that the reason they stress the importance of sharing the power in their relationship is to keep their relationship from becoming tyrannical. At first Ted felt threatened by the fact that Nancy was questioning his decision. However, he realized that there would come a time when he would strongly question one of her decisions, and he knew that he would want his voice to be heard in such a situation. As a result, Ted decided to give in to his wife, and told Julia that it was all right for her to go out with Ken.

Modes of Thought and Behavior

Individuals with a government story tend to have relationships that center on power relations. Thus, whereas distribution of power is an issue in every relationship, it is a more central issue in relationships with a government story.

Because there are so many variants of power distribution, there are many possible types of government stories. In the case of Nancy and Ted, for example, a power-sharing arrangement that generally has worked smoothly breaks down when one partner comes to perceive the other as having made an arbitrary decision. In this particular case, the other partner accommodates. Not all partners do, of course, which can lead to conflict.

Jerry and Kristen do not have the kind of distributed power-sharing arrangement that Nancy and Ted have. Instead, Kristen has arrogated most of the power in the relationship. Jerry finds himself telling friends that he is too busy to bother with relationship decisions. He may feel that way, or he may have convinced himself he does, or he may be telling his friends something that he does not believe himself. In this last case, Jerry may have a need for submission, which is more or less what would be required in order to maintain the relationship as it is over any long period of time.[2]

Sometimes, in the early phases of a relationship, people are able to tolerate behavior that later on they will find intolerable. The imbalance is strong enough in the case of Jerry and Kristen that one cannot help wondering whether this relationship can last. Whether it does or not depends on whether Jerry really wants to be dominated, or instead is putting up with domination because he is sufficiently in love with Kristen that he chooses not to contest the issue.

The problem with not contesting the issue, if it is indeed an issue, is that a precedent is established. Power, once ceded, can be hard to retrieve, as many government leaders have found out. It is therefore probably a poor idea to cede power in a relationship in the hope that it later can be recovered. The recovery can prove very hard to accomplish, and moreover, the other partner may feel that if the arrangement was unsatisfactory, the dissatisfied individual should have said so in the first place.

Complementary Roles: Governor and Governed, Power Sharers, Power Avoiders

The three main pairs of shared roles are quite different in various versions of the government story. In the governor-governed (autocratic) relationship, one individual takes on most of the power in the relationship, with or without the agreement of the other partner. In the power-sharing (democratic) arrangement, power is more or less equally divided, although it may be distributed differently across domains (e.g., financial control versus control of children). In the power-avoidant relationship, a somewhat anarchic situation exists in which neither individual wants to take power or responsibility. In the examples cited earlier, Kristen is the governor and Jerry is the governed; Nancy and Ted are power sharers, but a decision of Ted's that seemed arbitrary has forced a redefinition of the power-sharing arrangement.

Advantages and Disadvantages

The greatest advantage of the government story is that it makes explicit an issue that is implicit in any relationship: All relationships involve allocations of power.[3] These allocations are clearer in government-driven relationships than in other kinds. By bringing power issues out into the open, these relationships may avoid problems that other relationships face as they struggle to figure out that power distribution is a problem, albeit a hidden one.

The most apparent potential disadvantage of government relationships is that power issues can start to take over the entire relationship. The partners can become so obsessed with issues of who has what power that they stop facing other issues and stop enjoying other aspects of the relationship.

Autocratic relationships can potentially open the door to abuse, especially if the autocrat begins to see him-or herself as literally all-powerful. If power corrupts, and absolute power corrupts absolutely, then couples in an autocratic relationship are at great risk. In many cases of abuse, abusers believe that they are perfectly within their rights to do whatever they want. Laws in some societies actually support this view.

In anarchic relationships, things can also get out of control, but in this case it is because no one is taking adequate responsibility for anything. The result can be destroyed finances, children with no one to look after them, and a disordered relationship on top of it all.

Anarchic relationships illustrate that some kind of governing principles are needed for any relationship. Ignoring the issue of what these principles will be does not result in the issue's going away.

☞ THE POLICE STORY

One does not have to be a police officer to think like one. People with a police story think like a police officer, but not just any kind of police officer. Instead, they think like the kind of police officer represented by Javert in *Les Misérables*. Javert sees things in black and white. There is right and wrong, and Javert believes that he represents what is right. Eventually, when he ceases to be able to fit events into his worldview, he kills himself rather than change this view.

Police officers in relationships view it as their responsibility to enforce the laws of the relationship, which they often view as coming from some kind of natural or societal law, but which, more typically, are of their own creation. The laws may more or less correspond to the laws of society (such as "outlawing" bigamy, incest, adultery, or whatever), or the laws may be bizarre creations of the police officer (for example, "outlawing" a woman's socializing in any way with a man, or outlawing a man's working with a woman, even in the course of his professional responsibilities).

The person who becomes involved in such a relationship may not realize what he or she has gotten into until things are quite far along. What at first may seem like small peculiarities in the partner begin to add up, but by the time the partner realizes what is going on, he or she may find the police officer as difficult to shake as Javert was for Jean Valjean. The police officer may invent punishments for infractions of the laws, and in cases of perceptions of extreme violation of these laws, the safety of the police officer's partner may be in jeopardy. In relationships, as in actual policing, the line between the law enforcer and the lawbreaker can become fuzzy, and the police officer granted too much power may find her- or himself becoming the lawbreaker.

For the person who is the recipient of what can become unwanted attention, the police story can share some attributes of the horror story, which will be discussed later in this section. The greatest difference is the police officer's feeling of absolute moral justification. The perpetrator of the horror story may well view him- or herself as having "unusual tastes." The police officer views him- or herself as similar to an officer of the law—upholding right, even sometimes to the point of committing serious wrongs in its name.

Diagnosing the Police Story

OFFICER

1 I believe it is necessary to watch your partner's every move to maintain some degree of order in your relationship.
2 I believe that in relationships you invariably need to keep a close eye on your partner.
3 I believe it is foolish to let your guard down and to trust your partner completely.
4 I would never trust my partner in a situation in which he or she would work closely with a person of the opposite sex.

SUSPECT

1 My partner often calls me several times during the day to ask exactly what I am doing.
2 My partner keeps close tabs on me.
3 My partner needs to know everything that I do.
4 My partner gets very upset if I don't let him or her know exactly where I have been.

Walter and Tracy

It is almost impossible for Walter to do anything in his life without his wife, Tracy, having to know and approve of it. At the dinner table, she makes sure that he is eating right; before he goes to work, she makes sure that he is dressed properly; before he goes out with his friends, she wants to know where he is going and what time he will be returning.

Walter's friends think that Walter is crazy for putting up with this kind of treatment, but there is a part of him that desires to be kept under such close surveillance. Maybe it is because his mother was very strict with him while he was growing up; or perhaps it is because he has always felt a little insecure, and having someone take such a strong interest in his life makes him feel better about himself. Either way, Walter does not regard Tracy's persistent vigilance as a negative aspect of the relationship, although sometimes he feels more constrained than he would like.

At times, Walter develops a greater desire for freedom, and asks Tracy to let down her watchfulness over him. Usually Tracy gives in to these rare requests for freedom, but occasionally they make her very suspicious. If she gives in, it is likely to be for a brief period; or worse, at times she pretends to give in, but only to create the opportunity to see what Walter will do when he thinks he is free from surveillance.

After one such request, Tracy started to think that Walter's desire for freedom meant that he was having an affair with someone at work. Her suspicion was fueled by a television program in which a husband cheated on his wife. In the hours following the show, Tracy became more and more certain of her suspicion; by the time Walter came home from work, she was so convinced that Walter was sleeping with another woman that she was ready to throw something at him the moment he walked through the door.

When Walter saw his wife in such a state, he had no idea what to do. Tracy accused Walter of having an affair, and he denied everything vehemently; after all, he had never done anything even remotely like what Tracy was accusing him of. Nevertheless, Tracy continued to shout at him, describing in almost gruesome detail her interpretation of the situation. Walter repeatedly told her that she could call anyone she wanted to at his office to verify his innocence, but he eventually saw that Tracy's suspicions were impervious to reason. She had been suspicious of him before, but never had it been so intense.

In situations like this one, Walter's patience with Tracy's watchfulness wears thin. However, Walter's requests for freedom are so infrequent that incidents such as this one rarely arise. Moreover, Tracy's watchfulness gives him a curious sense of satisfaction over the fact that anyone could care so much about him and what he does. For the most part, Walter enjoys Tracy's watchfulness. Thus, despite the disbelief of his friends, Walter swears that there is nothing wrong with having someone make sure that he is eating right, dressing properly, and getting home at a reasonable hour.

Becky and Dan

When Becky first started going out with Dan three years ago, she thought that she had met the perfect man. He was good-looking and intelligent; even more important, he seemed to care a lot about her. From the outset, he was always commenting on her appearance as well as inquiring into her interests and hobbies. At first Becky was flattered by the strong interest Dan had in her life; although he would occasionally make fun of what she was wearing or tease her about one of her hobbies, he was usually quite complimentary both of her and of her actions. But then things started to change.

After a while, Dan's occasional jokes became more frequent, and sometimes turned into scathing criticisms. Almost immediately, Becky started to become extremely self-conscious of everything that she said or did around Dan. She didn't want to slip up, even in small ways.

As time went on, Dan began to criticize Becky more and more, pointing out flaws in what seemed to be just about every aspect of her life. Moreover, he seemed always to want to keep track of her entire schedule, down to the most insignificant details. At this point, Becky and Dan had moved in with each other, and at times Becky felt as though she were in prison, with Dan as the warden. Whenever she would express her concerns, however, Dan would just tell her that he thought it was very important that he always know what she was doing—for her own good. Moreover, he pointed out that if he was criticizing her too much, it was only because he loved her and wanted her to be the best person she could be.

Although Becky knew that Dan was being sincere, she had trouble understanding how his trenchant critique of her was a result of his love. His steady barrage of criticisms ranged from suggestions to lose some weight to requests to dress more appropriately and even to admonitions that watching too much television would rot her mind and later make her unfit for being a proper mother. Nevertheless, Becky continued to tolerate Dan's behavior, because despite everything she loved him. She still wanted to hold on to her wavering trust in his assurance that his criticisms were simply a part of his love for her.

Recently, however, Dan's close inspections of Becky's appearance and behavior have gotten completely out of hand. He has become extremely intense in his interest in Becky's life, especially regarding the "flirtatious" and even "promiscuous" behavior he insists that she exhibits in public. Every time she shows an interest in what any other male is saying, Dan seems to think that she is planning to leave him for this man. Becky must always be on guard to make certain that she is not doing anything that Dan might construe as a flirtatious act. And with Dan, it doesn't take much for an act to be construed as flirtatious.

As Dan and Becky get ready to go out to dinner with the Johnsons tonight, Becky is putting on her least revealing dress and is continually reminding herself not to get too personal with Doug Johnson. But she now feels that she never can predict what will set Dan off.

Despite Becky's preparation and determined efforts to be on her best behavior throughout the dinner, Dan still reprimands her for acting flirtatiously. She insists that she was behaving appropriately, but Dan will not listen to her, sticking to his belief that Becky is thinking about leaving him. Dan's face is red with anger as he warns her that any further flirtations will have to result in consequences for her.

Modes of Thought and Behavior

The key feature of the police story is the unremitting surveillance that is directed by one partner toward the other. This surveillance goes beyond the usual interest in a partner's activities, and beyond any kind of reasonable interest in the partner's welfare. The interest is driven by a seemingly unquenchable need for control that reduces the partner to a humiliating role, almost without regard to what the partner does.

Studies done at Stanford University showed that if people are arbitrarily assigned roles of prison guards and prisoners and then placed in a situation in which they enact these roles, the persons assigned to be prison guards become more and more authoritarian toward their "prisoners," and less and less humane in their treatment of them. The prisoners, in turn, start to fulfill the roles of prisoners and begin to feel the kind of humiliation and degradation that goes with being incarcerated.[1]

The police story can start off being one person's story and end up being both persons' story, almost without the second partner even realizing what is happening. As the second partner more and more plays the role of suspect, or even of prisoner, the role can become self-confirming and take on a kind of bizarre reality—as though one deserves to be suspected of various crimes. As the story unfolds, it can become increasingly divorced from any kind of reality in which anyone besides the couple can share. And as many partners of police officers have discovered the hard way, it can be extremely hard to escape the reality. Some people, like Walter, may actually enjoy being in the role of suspect, relishing, perhaps, the attention they get in no other aspect of their life. Others, like Becky, may find themselves uncomfortable with the role, but unsure of what they can do to escape from it.

Complementary Roles: Police Officer and Suspect

The complementary roles in the police story are the police officer and the suspect (who sometimes becomes the prisoner). Although the roles may alternate, typically one person fulfills the role of police officer, while the other is the suspect. The roles may deepen and broaden with time, meaning that more and more of the suspect's behavior comes to be viewed as suspicious or as downright "illegal." Attempts by the suspect to escape the role are often viewed as another crime—that of the prisoner trying to escape his or her punishment. To the police office, the ultimate crime is the attempt to free oneself of the relationship.

The behavior of the self-appointed police officer may actually foment exactly the behavior on the part of the partner that the police officer is attempting to suppress. The suspect, suspected or even convicted of a crime he or she did not commit, may no longer see the value of not committing it. After all, he or she will be treated as guilty regardless of whether he or she has committed the crime, so why not commit it? Or the person may internalize the view of him- or herself projected by the police officer, and thereby start to act in the ways that are expected of him or her.

Police officers in relationships, as in the everyday world, may come to see themselves as above their own laws. They may view abuse as a legitimate form of punishment, and even murder as a legitimate form of execution. In a twisted way, they may come to see themselves as persecuted by the crimes of the victim.

Some high-profile cases that end up in the (real) courts have elements of a police story. For example, the relationship between O. J. Simpson and his wife, Nicole Brown Simpson, seems to have borne elements—such as unremitting surveillance and punishment—of a police story, although, of course, one cannot make a compelling judgment on the basis of media reports.

Advantages and Disadvantages

Police stories do not have very favorable prognoses because of their susceptibility to continued escalation and departure from any kind of adaptive reality. The police story may have, for some people, the kind of positive aspect it had for Walter—the feeling of being cared for. People who are very insecure may relish the attention that they are unable to receive in any other way. But they can end up paying a steep price. The story is engrossing, but may turn dangerous.

The greatest disadvantage is that as the plot thickens, the suspect first begins to lose freedom, then dignity, and then any kind of self-respect. Eventually, the person's mental and even physical well-being may come to be threatened. Meanwhile, the police officer may be departing farther and farther from any kind of tenable reality without ever realizing what is happening. What starts off as a fairly routine and harmless police story can degenerate over time into a paranoid fantasy, damaging both participants in the story.

☞ THE PORNOGRAPHY STORY

The pornography story is a story of degradation and debasement. The individual with the pornography story either sees love as debasement and finds it difficult, if not impossible, to love someone without debasing that person, or else the person wishes to be debased. The passion in the relationship is generated by the debasement, and one can argue over whether what the individual is experiencing is love, in any meaningful sense of the word. For the person with this story, it is usually the only kind of love he or she knows.

The debasement can happen within the context of the primary relationship, or in the context of one or more secondary ones. If, for whatever reason, the person does not want to or is unable to debase the primary partner, or, in the case of the complementary role, is not debased by the partner, he or she is likely to go looking elsewhere, perhaps while maintaining the primary relationship.

Although our research shows that few people of either sex admit to a pornography story, this story is almost certainly much more common than people wish to admit.[1] The thriving prostitution trade, number of books and movies based on this story, and the market for forms of sex that debase partners (such as by threatening them, whipping them, chaining them, or mutilating them) suggest that this story is more widespread than one might imagine. Nor does it show any signs of being on the decline.

Diagnosing the Pornography Story

OBJECT

1 The truth is that I don't mind being treated as a sex toy by my partner.

2 I confess that it is very important to me to be able to gratify all my partner's sexual desires and whims, even if other people might view them as debasing me.

3 I get bored when I am with a partner who does not want me to be adventurous in a pornographic sort of a way in my sexual relations with him or her.

4 I like it when my partner wants me to try new and unusual, and even painful, sexual techniques.

SUBJECT

1 I like to use a variety of sexual techniques, especially ones that most other people would view as bizarre or even degrading toward my partner.

2 The most important thing to me in my relationship is for my partner to be an excellent sex toy, doing anything that I desire.

3 I can never be happy with a partner who is not very adventurous, in a pornographic sort of a way, in his or her sex life.

4 The truth is that I like a partner who feels like a sex object.

Ray and Tiffany

Ray stares across the bar at Tiffany, eyeing her seductively until she meets his gaze. His look makes her feel uneasy, and so she turns away from him. Although she is unsettled, she is drawn to him, and is soon compelled to look back. When she does, Ray is still staring at her, stirring his drink with a straw. Ray's look makes Tiffany feel cheap; she can sense that his interest in her is purely sexual. She feels as though he is the hunter and she is the prey, waiting to be captured. Although this feeling disgusts her, she cannot deny some part of herself that desires to be caught by him and service his every whim.

Ray notices Tiffany's uneasiness as well as her submissiveness; he moves over toward her slowly, with his eyes fixed on hers. When Tiffany sees that he is coming, she turns away and stares at the wall, but she does not move. She starts breathing more heavily as he approaches. Soon he is upon her, and without saying a word, he sweeps two of his fingers along her cheek and through her hair. She swallows nervously but does not say a word; the more impersonal the better. Ray gently moves his fingers down along Tiffany's neck and shoulder. Sensing her quivering body, he feels a rush of excitement. They begin kissing, breathing heavily as they do so; Ray teases her, backing up every once in a while to stare at her with a sly grin. Finally he turns around and begins walking toward the door.

After a few steps, he looks back at Tiffany and, with a slight twitch of his head, motions her to follow him. Tiffany glances nervously around the room, wondering if anyone is watching them—part of her hoping that there is, part of her ashamed to feel this way. She follows Ray out the door and into his car. Still without exchanging a word, they drive over to Ray's apartment. When they arrive, they walk straight to the bedroom. Ray starts taking Tiffany's clothes off and places her on the bed, but he does not join her. Instead, he watches as she shivers in anticipation, waiting for his next move. Her heart begins to beat even faster as he reaches into a drawer and pulls out a pair of handcuffs.

Tiffany wakes up the next morning to find herself alone in Ray's bed. She is ashamed of herself but understands that she has almost no control over her need to be treated this way. She is drawn to men like Ray—men who do not care about her as a person and think of her only as a sexual object to be captured and debased. She notices a piece of paper on a night table beside the bed; on it there is no name or number, only an address and a time. Presumably this is where Ray wants to meet her again. Tiffany gets up, takes a shower, puts on her clothes, and leaves. Even after the shower, she still feels dirty.

Knowing herself, she realizes that she will probably wind up in the spot Ray jotted down, and at just the requested time, too; but she also recognizes that it would be better for her to stay away. She has been in situations like this one before, and she knows the course they usually take. The relationship almost never gets beyond the impersonal, purely physical aspects. Moreover, the thrill provided by the early sexual experiences fades quickly, and to maintain the high level of excitement, the sex has to become rougher and rougher; the need to debase, on the one hand, and to be debased, on the other, keeps escalating until potentially dangerous means of extracting excitement have to come into play. Soon they take over the whole relationship. Tiffany realizes that, in all honesty, they are the whole relationship.

Tiffany never wants the relationships to get out of hand in this way, but she knows that once she gets involved in them, her sense of reason and of what is reasonable starts to fail. She is swept away by what seem to her to be primal needs. As she stares at the piece of paper in her hand, she desperately wishes she could tear it up, but she feels compelled to hold on to it, and to meet Ray when and where he wants her to.

Carol and Tim

Carol is tired of playing the role of the trophy—the beautiful woman who is always accompanying some rich man around town while being treated like an object. She is determined to reverse the situation, just to see what the other side is like. So tonight she will go into town and pick out the sexiest, yet most innocent and vulnerable, young male that she can find.

After debating with herself, she decides to go to Dean's Place, a dance club notorious for its lecherous atmosphere. Once she arrives, she moves immediately into a corner, seeking to get a good view of the entire place. She shrugs off all the men who come over to her; after all, she wants to initiate everything. Eventually she notices someone sitting by the bar; he is young and handsome, but more important, he has that vulnerable look that Carol wants more than anything else. She walks over to him and offers to buy him a drink.

The young man is slightly mystified by her forward approach but accepts her offer and introduces himself as Tim. Carol can tell by his clothes and his style that he is not very rich, which pleases her, because she imagines his lower economic status will enhance his role as an object for her. She invites him to dinner, and although Tim is still somewhat baffled by the whole situation, he gladly accepts her invitation.

Two days pass, and Carol and Tim's date is only minutes away. Carol picks up Tim at his house and is pleased to see that he is dressed down in jeans and a flannel shirt. She is wearing a very fancy dress, and believes the contrast should make Tim feel even more vulnerable. They go to a restaurant of Carol's choice—a fancy Italian place where she knows the owner. As they walk up to the entrance, Carol sees the owner standing by the door and gives him a kiss and a hug, paying close attention to Tim's awkward stance beside her. She is definitely getting off on the experience.

After being seated, Carol tells Tim that she will order for both of them. She does not want him to have a say in anything; she just wants him to sit there—a beautiful, helpless face for all to see.

As the night progresses, Carol can see that her efforts to make Tim feel insecure are working quite well. She becomes quite aroused when she thinks of how effectively she has degraded him, and of what she still has in store for him later in the evening. At the end of the meal, Carol offers to pay the check, and then asks Tim if he would like to come over to her place; Tim simply nods at this point. They leave the restaurant and drive back to Carol's apartment.

On the drive home, Carol moves her hand up and down Tim's thigh; he can only manage a slight smile. After all, he is having trouble deciding if he is involved in a fantasy or a nightmare in disguise. When they arrive at Carol's apartment, they go immediately to the bedroom, where Carol places him seductively on the bed. She grabs a handkerchief from a drawer and asks him—or, more appropriately, tells him—to use it as a blindfold.

By the time Carol and Tim have been seeing each other for three weeks, Tim is already starting to have doubts. All along he has been aware of his role in the relationship, and although he is not particularly proud of it, there is a part of him that has always enjoyed being cheapened in this manner. Even though Carol has taken an interest in him, he knows that this interest is nothing more than the arousal she feels in degrading him. Moreover, he knows that if the relationship is to last, Carol will need continually to make increased efforts to debase him. After a while, these efforts will probably lead the relationship absolutely nowhere. Tim knows he should get out; he just isn't ready to leave the relationship quite yet, and isn't sure when he will be ready.

Modes of Thought and Behavior

To love, in this story, is to debase or be debased. Love is dirty, and without the dirt, it's just not appealing. This view is at the same time both supported and rejected by society. People with a pornography story thereby find themselves in the curious position of having a story that is continually being portrayed in various media as unacceptable but nevertheless as titillating and maybe even fun. It's a story you're supposed to have if you want a story you're not supposed to have. And the simultaneous attraction and repulsion of society to this story is part of what makes it so exciting, yet so ambiguous in character.

People with a pornography story may marry someone who plays into that story, but more likely they will marry someone who does not fit the story at all—giving them social respectability—and then play out the story elsewhere. This social respectability is not necessarily a deceit or for others' eyes only. It may be for their own eyes as well. They may have a bifurcated view whereby marriage is for respectability—which they crave—but other relationships are for dirt, which they crave even more. In other cases, they may be able to find, in the same relationship, both social respectability and, in the privacy of the bedroom, debasement.

This story, like the police story or the horror story, tends to feed on itself. What is sufficient to achieve some kind of arousal one day may not be sufficient the next, and people like Tim, who worry as to where it will all lead, are probably well advised to be concerned. Once habituation and boredom set in, the only options are to leave the relationship—which has started to lose its interest—or to increase its pornographic content. Eventually the pornographic content may get out of control, as occasional newspaper stories remind us when a participant accidentally is killed when things go wrong. Tiffany recognizes that her relationship with Ray can only go downhill, but as is usually the case in these relationships, it is one thing to know something, another to act on it.

Complementary Roles: Subject and Object

There are two roles in a pornography story—subject and object—but people may reverse roles, as in the story of Carol and Tim. Carol, fed up with being the object, becomes the subject. The curious thing about these relationships is just how ambiguous the roles are: When one debases another, one debases oneself. And allowing another person to debase oneself also results in one's debasing the other. At some level, therefore, there is a certain duality in the roles played out in this story.

People playing out the pornography story want to make another person feel worthless, in what is usually a vain attempt to make themselves feel a sense of worth. But it's never enough, precisely because debasement is not ultimately going to lead anyone to feel a sense of worth. Instead of seeking other means to acquire self-worth, however, debasers are likely to fortify their attempts to debase others, always with the same results, and always with the dissatisfaction that they have not fully accomplished what they had hoped to.

Advantages and Disadvantages

If there are any advantages to the pornography story, they are not obvious. The disadvantages are quite clear, however. First, the excitement people attain is through degradation of themselves and others. Second, the need to debase and be debased is likely to keep escalating. Third, once one adopts the story, it may be difficult to adopt another story. Fourth, the story can become physically as well as psychologically dangerous. And finally, no matter how one tries, it is difficult to turn the story into an adaptive one in terms of any kind of psychological or physical well-being. But stories are stories, not subject to any kind of rational logic, and many of the people engaged in the pornography story pursue it even while knowing all its disadvantages to themselves and their partners.

☞ THE HORROR STORY

In the horror story the relationship is appealing to an individual because he or she either is terrorizing a partner or is being terrorized by a partner. The individuals like to scare, or to be scared of, their partner. The novel *Looking for Mr. Goodbar* (later a movie) recounted the story of a woman whose horror story eventually led to her death. Of course, sometimes people unwittingly end up in horror stories, as in the movie *Fatal Attraction*.

People with horror stories typically view themselves as having anything but a horror story. Those who prefer the role of terrorizer tend to see themselves as liking to have a little fun, or as liking to make life interesting for themselves and their partner, or as liking rough sex, or as falling for people who are "asking for it." Those who prefer the role of victim tend to consider themselves as un-lucky—always somehow ending up with the wrong person—or as good-natured people who are therefore easy prey for exploiters, or as being too nice. Neither the terrorizer's self-image nor the victim's bears much resemblance to the behavioral reality. The fact that peo-ple keep ending up in these relationships suggests that more than chance factors are operating.

What are the factors in people's backgrounds that are likely to lead them into horror-story relationships? One common factor ap-pears to be models of aggression and abuse, often in the parental home. High levels of unrestrained aggression or abject submission in role models are also common. Movie and television scripts can help reinforce these models, leading to a form of social learning whereby the individuals come to imitate or to want to imitate the behavior they are observing.[1] Another common factor is the need for power on the part of the terrorizer, or the need for submission or debase-ment on the part of the victim.[2] Environmental factors interact with personality factors to produce this story, just as is the case with any other story.

Whether a horror story emerges in a relationship depends not just on the interaction of early environment with personality; how a particular relationship interacts with these factors is important, too. Someone for whom a horror story is somewhat foreign may find the story emerging if the individual is paired with a person for whom this story predominates. Such a person may invite—explicitly or implicitly—abusive behavior, which leads to a pattern of abuse that the partner would not have fallen into with another person. As the pattern emerges, the story may overshadow other stories in a hierarchy to the point where it becomes dominant.

The research of Stanley Milgram showed that ordinary people could be made to behave in ways that were surprisingly like those of the Nazis during World War II. People of various kinds were brought into a laboratory and were incited to show blind obedience to the commands of an experimenter that resulted in their administering what they believed to be painful and even potentially lethal shocks to another individual (who was, unbeknownst to the participants, a confederate of the experimenter).[3] The relevance of Milgram's work for us here is that even people who thought that they could never become involved in a horrific, abusive relationship can find themselves unwittingly sucked into one, which can then become a pattern in their life.

Diagnosing the Horror Story

TERRORIZER

1 I often make sure that my partner knows that I am in charge, even if it involves having my partner being scared of me.
2 I actually find it exciting when I feel my partner is somewhat frightened of me.
3 I don't think there is anything wrong with having your partner be slightly scared of you.
4 I sometimes do things that scare my partner, because I think it is actually good for a relationship to have one partner slightly frightened of the other.

VICTIM

1   I believe it is somewhat exciting to be slightly scared of your partner.

2   I find it arousing when my partner creates a sense of fear in me.

3   I keep getting into relationships with people who could have come right out of a horror story.

4   I tend to end up with people who sometimes frighten me.

Sally and Mark

Sally is a waitress at a local diner. Late one night she notices someone staring at her from a booth. From the moment she first lays eyes on the man, she knows that there is something different about him, although she is not able to pinpoint exactly what it is. Sally feels slightly uncomfortable being stared at like this, but the man seems harmless, and beyond that, she finds him very attractive. When she goes to pick up his tip, she sees that there is a name and a telephone number on one of the bills. The man's name is Mark, and after Sally gets off work, she gives him a call.

Mark asks her if she wants to go to *The Texas Chainsaw Massacre* with him. She would prefer to see another kind of movie but he tells her how much he wants to see it, and so she agrees to go. Throughout the movie, she notices that whenever she looks away from a violent scene, Mark flashes her a smile. She has the feeling that Mark has seen this movie before, perhaps multiple times. She also believes that he is merely making fun of her for her fear; she has no idea that it is a smile of excitement.

Before she knows it, Sally has been seeing Mark for three weeks. One night, when the two of them return to Mark's house after a night on the town, Sally tells Mark that she wants to spend the weekend with some of her friends at the beach. Upon hearing this, Mark becomes very silent, and his hands begin to shake. Sally is very frightened by this behavior and does not know what to do. Mark finally breaks the silence, asking Sally why she wants to leave him.

Sally responds by saying that she will be gone only for the weekend, and that they can do something together the moment she returns. Mark only seems to get angrier at this response, and he tells her that he forbids her to leave. Sally begins to make a response, but before she can get a word out, Mark grabs her by the shoulders and presses down upon them, despite her pleas to let her go. With wide, glaring eyes, he tells her never to say anything that makes him angry. Shaking uncontrollably underneath the pressure of his hands, Sally mutters, almost to herself, that she will never do it again. Mark finds Sally's fear arousing, and he begins to kiss her neck, breathing heavily as he does so.

Despite this incident, Sally does not break up with Mark. Perhaps it is because she is afraid of what he might do to her if she leaves him, or maybe it is because in some odd way she is drawn to Mark— a man for whom a relationship can be interesting only if his partner is genuinely afraid of him. Whatever the explanation, Sally's relationship with Mark continues.

Keith and Elise

Keith met Elise at a bar. He was sitting by himself when she came over to him and asked if he would like to be her partner in her upcoming pool match. Keith told Elise that he was not a very good pool player, but she said that it did not matter. Keith was intrigued by the cool, calm way that Elise was speaking to him, so he decided to take her up on her offer. Despite Keith's poor playing, the two of them kept defeating one team after the other, due to Elise's immense talents. Keith was very impressed, and realized that he was beginning to fall for Elise. They arranged to meet the next night, and before long they were seeing each other on a regular basis.

Keith enjoyed spending time with Elise, but after a while he started to feel a little uneasy around her. The cool, calm style that she conveyed on the night they met—the style that had drawn him to her—was no front; she was almost completely unflappable. Actually, it seemed as though Elise never got angry, never got sad, and never got happy either.

A few nights ago, while Elise and Keith were kissing each other on Elise's bed, Elise suddenly backed away from Keith and turned to pick up a candle from the dresser. In her unshakably calm voice, she asked Keith to put his hand over it. Keith could not believe that she was serious, and let out a slight laugh. Without any anger, she grabbed his arm and brought his hand toward the flame. Keith is not a very strong man and was unable to remove his arm from Elise's tight grip. He began shouting at her, but she did not heed his screams, bringing his hand closer to the flame. The most terrifying aspect of it all was the eerie serenity of Elise's expression during this act; in fact, she almost seemed aroused by his fear. As the heat from the candle began to burn his hand, Keith swung his free arm and dislodged the candle from Elise's grasp. He moved into the corner of the room, and Elise started to walk slowly toward him. Terrified of Elise's oncoming figure, Keith scampered quickly by her, running into the living room and out of the house. He got into his car and quickly drove home. When he arrived at his apartment, he went straight to his bed and wrapped himself in the covers.

The next morning, Keith woke up to the sound of a ringing telephone. He picked up the receiver to hear Elise's voice on the other end. She apologized for what she had done to him, and she asked him to meet her at the local diner. Keith was pretty certain that Elise's apology was not completely sincere and that the behavior she had exhibited on the previous night most likely would resurface at some point in the future. After all, this was not the first time that he had been involved in a relationship in which his partner had taken pleasure in frightening him, and so he knew what to expect. Nevertheless, he agreed to meet Elise at the diner, because, for whatever reason, he seems always to be drawn to these types of relationships. Keith finds himself looking forward to seeing Elise, and wondering what she will do to him next.

Modes of Thought and Behavior

People who are attracted to a horror story can have a variety of distinctive perceptions of the kind of story their relationships represent. Abused individuals, often but not always women, may sense a horror story for what it is and, as in the case of Sally, be afraid to leave because the consequences of leaving seem potentially more dangerous than the consequences of staying. Given the very weak and sketchy laws that exist for dealing with abusers, and the spotty nature of their enforcement, the victims, unfortunately, often prove to be right.

In general, different love stories are just that—different; they are not "good" or "bad." But a horror story comes about as close as one can get to a story that is bad, or at the very least maladaptive, for a variety of reasons.

First, when the story is not mutual, the one who does not share it too often becomes trapped in it, as is probably the case with Sally. The trap may be because of a fear of physical harm, or because the given societal customs allow the horrors to take place, or because the partner cannot survive on his or her own financially, or because family pressure impels the person to stay in the abusive relationship. Sally, for example, feels trapped and unable to leave what for her has become an awful relationship, because she is afraid of what Mark might do.

Second, horror stories are unusually susceptible to the kind of escalation that results in physical harm to one or both participants. Keith, for example, is asking for trouble, and will probably get it. It is not always the victim who gets hurt, however. Sometimes the formerly passive victim turns on the terrorizer, leaving the terrorizer as the one who is physically harmed. The case of John and Lorena Bobbitt comes to mind as a fairly extreme example: Lorena Bobbitt, after what she described as years of severe abuse, finally rebelled and severed her husband's penis.

Third, relationships that start off as being about another story sometimes convert to a horror story. When they do, it is almost always the result of a degenerative process in the relationship. The couple may find themselves becoming increasingly antagonistic, or, as so often happens, one partner may not accept the other's desire to end the relationship (as in the events portrayed in *Fatal Attraction*). This partner then enters a horror story in which the other partner probably wishes to have no part. Indeed, in such cases, the partner may have no desire to be a part of any story at all that involves the ex-lover.

Fourth, horror stories can involve increasing amounts of degradation. Terrorizers may start to find that, after a while, the depredations that once gave them a thrill no longer do. They may find themselves becoming habituated to the level of terror they elicit, and need to provoke greater and greater levels of terror in the victim in order to satisfy themselves.

Complementary Roles: Terrorizer and Victim

The complementary roles in the horror story are terrorizer and victim. In seeking partners, terrorizers look for individuals who will be afraid of them and who will succumb to their terrors. Victims look for partners who will terrorize them. The two roles are generally not interchangeable: Terrorizers do not want to be victims, and victims do not want to be terrorizers.

People who enter a horror story often have a cover story for why they tend to get into the relationships they do. The terrorizer is likely to report that the victim got what he or she (more often, she) "asked for" or "deserved," whereas the victim is likely to view himself or herself as unlucky, or to view members of the opposite sex as all closet bastards or bitches who, given the opportunity, would terrorize anyone.

The horror story can be situational rather than dispositional, as many people who have been involved in a dissolving relationship can report. Psychologists have found that certain situations can have very powerful effects on behavior with the result that people who thought themselves to be perfectly ordinary, or even more calm than most, may find themselves in a degenerating spiral.[4] In such a spiral, the actions of one partner invite retaliation, which comes, only to be followed by further retaliation, and so on until the situation reels out of control.

Because stories are such powerful forces, people for whom the horror story is not particularly attractive may find the story taking on significance as the partner acts more and more in ways that invite the partner to play the role of terrorizer or victim. In order to stop the progression, the partner needs, first, to realize what is happening; second, to want to do something about it; third, to know what to do about it; and fourth, actually to do it, risking unpredictable consequences. For example, someone for whom the horror story is actually frightening may inadvertently end up in a relationship with a terrorizer, and then find herself thinking more and more like a victim. Step by step, the role may take over, leaving the individual in a fright from which there seems no good escape. Sometimes there isn't.

Advantages and Disadvantages

The horror story probably is the least adaptive and advantageous of the stories considered in this book. To some, it may be exciting. But the forms of terror needed to sustain the excitement may keep escalating, eventually achieving dangerous levels. Horror stories tend to get out of control and to put their participants, and even sometimes those around them, at both psychological and physical risk. Those who discover themselves either to have this story or to be in a relationship that is enacting it would be well advised to seek counseling, and perhaps even police protection.

OBJECT STORIES

In object stories, either persons or relationships become valued not for themselves, but for their functioning as objects. It often seems as though the particular person or relationship matters little, so long as certain functions are being carried out.

PERSON AS OBJECT

In stories of persons as objects, the person fulfills a role of object. In a science-fiction story, the person is valued for his or her bizarre character or behavior. In a collection story, the person is valued for filling a slot in a larger collection. In an art story, the person is valued for his or her physical appearance.

☞ THE SCIENCE-FICTION STORY

People with a science-fiction story either feel like they keep ending up with partners who are about as strange as a partner can possibly be, or feel themselves to be exceedingly strange and different from others and want to be with someone who values their extreme strangeness.

In the former case, two scenarios are common. Although both are science-fiction stories, they play out very differently. In one scenario, the individual consciously and purposely chooses people who seem strange. Part of the excitement of the relationship is in choosing the weirdest person one can find. An individual who does this may or may not want to accept that this tendency exists, but he or she is aware that it does.

In the second scenario, the person is perplexed as to why he or she keeps ending up with weirdoes. The individual may feel as though he or she makes sensible choices, only to see them turn out to be anything but sensible. Individuals in this category may start out being perplexed, but then become upset, outraged, or even bitter. They may feel that their partners are intentionally deceiving them, or at least holding back on their true nature. Communication is extremely important in relationships, but it is hard to communicate with someone who seems so alien.[1] They may also feel that they have very bad luck, always ending up with the strangest people imaginable.

In the second scenario, as in all scenarios for all stories, people not only select people to conform to their preferred story, but also actively shape the behavior of their partners. Thus, people who have a science-fiction story but are not at all aware of it may actually shape their partners' behavior toward weirdness, and then despair of how weirdly their partner behaves.

In the latter case, a person feels as though he or she has ended up on the wrong planet. The person experiences intense alienation from the society and the people it comprises. The individual thus seeks out someone who will be attracted to such unusual sentiments.

Diagnosing the Science-Fiction Story

1 I often find myself attracted to individuals who have unusual and strange characteristics, almost what you would expect of someone from another planet.
2 Sometimes my partner's behavior is so bizarre and unpredictable that I might almost wonder whether he or she is from this planet.
3 I am amazed at some people who claim to know their partner like a book, because I sometimes feel like my partner is an alien.
4 My partner is so unpredictable and strange that sometimes I have no clue about

what he or she might do next or whether he or she is even human in any meaningful sense of the word.

5   Sometimes it is beyond my comprehension why my partner acts the way he or she does: It is as if he or she has come out to a science-fiction book.

6   My partner baffles me so much that I sometimes feel that he or she could be from another planet.

7   I sometimes find my partner completely beyond comprehension; it is as if he or she is not from this world.

8   My partner is like an alien to me—incomprehensible and very strange.

Alexis and Ned

Alexis stares perplexedly at Ned, trying to comprehend what exactly he is babbling about as he drives her home along Sunset Boulevard. Fifteen minutes ago she asked him how he thought their relationship was going, and he has yet to finalize his answer. That in itself is not much of a problem; but the fact that his answer has very little to do with her question (at least from her perspective) is just another sign of Ned's extreme peculiarity.

When she asked the question, she expected that he would at least say something about his feelings toward her or make some sort of prediction as to where he thought the relationship might be heading; instead, he is telling her about the complexity of the human psyche and its emotions, and of his own inability to figure out what exactly he wants in this world. He cites passages from several of his favorite novels in an effort to help Alexis understand him better, but it is to no avail; the passages only make her more confused.

It would be one thing if Ned were simply avoiding her question, but Alexis knows that these really are his feelings. Ned is giving what he honestly believes to be a valid answer to Alexis's question. Frequently, he seems to be speaking in riddles to which there are no keys.

Alexis and Ned have been seeing each other for almost three months, and over that time Ned has not gotten any easier to understand. For a while Alexis felt that she was just not smart enough to understand Ned's complex thought processes. However, after countless conversations with him in which she unsuccessfully tried to figure out what he was saying, she became convinced that they are on two completely different wavelengths. She now believes that no increase in her intelligence would help her to understand him. As a result, it has not gotten any easier for her to communicate with him, and there are times when she wonders how he sees her fitting into his life. The fact that she still feels alienated from him in this way is preventing her from becoming more intimate with him.

Alexis wishes she could understand Ned better, because, despite his incomprehensibility, there are several things about him that she really likes. For one, there are times when he can be extremely romantic. One night he drove two hundred miles to pick her up unexpectedly from a business conference and take her to a candlelit dinner by the ocean. In addition, Ned often surprises Alexis with flowers or a small gift, and he has an uncanny way of knowing when she needs such a surprise to lift her spirits. Alexis only wishes that he occasionally would surprise her by making some sense for a change.

Albert and Frieda

Amid thousands of Neil Young fans, Albert and Frieda make their way to the parking lot. The concert has just ended and Frieda is trying to explain to Albert the meaning of Neil Young's music. She describes it as "spiritually transcendent, going beyond the normal sphere of humanity to a splendor that can only be reached through a sacrificial implosion of the soul." Albert nods, but with noticeable confusion; as usual, he has absolutely no idea of what Frieda is talking about.

Without paying any attention to Albert's response, or anything else, for that matter, Frieda goes on to describe Young's classic song "Heart of Gold" as "the artist's quest to forgo earthly pleasures and choose, rather, a life of torment, so as to achieve a supernatural oneness with death." Slightly amused by this impenetrable interpretation, Albert jokingly remarks that he is trying to avoid death for as long as possible. Frieda immediately turns on him, insisting that if he continues to make such asinine comments, she will never talk to him again.

Albert has been going out with Frieda for two and a half months, but he does not feel any closer to understanding her today than he did on the day they met. On the contrary, he is probably more puzzled by her now, simply because he has observed that much more of her behavior. The current Neil Young episode is just one of many such episodes in which Albert feels as if he were talking with someone from another planet.

Initially, Albert enjoyed Frieda's company; he was intrigued and amused by her oddities, and thought she was a very interesting woman, one he would like to get to know. After all, it is not often that he meets a person who is so different from all the rest. Moreover, he never knows what to expect from Frieda, and for a while there were many enjoyable surprises. One night they were driving into the city to see a movie when they realized that the starting time was a half hour later than they had thought. Without saying a word, Frieda took a detour to Bear Rock, a high perch from which people can see the entire city. When they arrived, Frieda leaned over to Albert, reclined his seat, and began kissing him. At first Albert felt a bit awkward about the whole situation, but after seeing that there was nobody around, he relaxed and had a wonderful time.

Recently, however, Albert has become frustrated with his inability to understand Frieda. It makes communicating with her almost impossible. It is as if they are speaking two different languages—only worse, because at least in that situation Albert could use a phrase book to translate. Whereas he originally was intrigued by Frieda's oddities, Albert is now mystified by them; he can never predict what she is going to do or say, and he never knows how she is going to respond to him. To illustrate, it has now been thirty minutes since they left the Neil Young concert, and Frieda is still fuming about Albert's joke regarding her analysis of "Heart of Gold." He is not sure whether he should apologize, bring up another topic, or just remain quiet; for all he knows, a seemingly innocuous change in conversation might bring about a total explosion on Frieda's part. He sees now that he will never be able to understand her. At the same time that he feels frustrated, though, he is utterly intrigued by Frieda and doesn't really want to leave her.

Modes of Thought and Behavior

People with a science-fiction story gravitate toward partners who are strange and incomprehensible to them—the more so, the better. Being "strange and incomprehensible" is, of course, a subjective judgment. Others may find the partners rather normal, or not very normal but easy to understand.

People with this story may view their partners much the way they would visitors from another planet. They may simultaneously feel both attraction and repulsion, or wonder why they are attracted to someone who is so strange. Or they may choose such persons and feel comfortable with the choice, enjoying the strangeness and recognizing that it is just what they seek in a partner.

People with a science-fiction story may have developed such a story, in part, as a rebellion against society. Often the partners they pick are the last ones their parents or others would like to see them with. The individuals they choose also tend to be counternormative, and may actually act in ways that the person with the science-fiction story would like to act but cannot bring him- or herself to.

The person who is perceived as the alien usually is unaware of the science-fiction story, because he or she typically does not share the view of him or herself as an alien. Indeed, the partner may feel that others, and even society as a whole, do not make sense, and that they are the only normal ones.

Complementary Roles: Alien and Human

The two complementary roles in the science-fiction story are the "alien" and the "human." The human perceives the partner as alien, but the alien does not perceive him- or herself in the same way.

Advantages and Disadvantages

Science-fiction stories have, as a positive feature, their surprise and sense of constant exploration. The person in the role of the human never quite understands the person in the role of the alien, and the alien may enjoy not being understood. The disadvantage, though, is that the story may become tiresome. The "human" may eventually conclude that the "alien" is resisting being understood, or just does not make any real sense, or is not worth understanding in the first place. The "alien," who may feel apart from society to begin with, may unknowingly relish not being understood, and may eventually conclude that the partner, like everyone else, just does not understand him or her. Thus, the potential for frustration is high for both partners.

A further disadvantage is that one may be making a choice only in terms of weirdness, and not in terms of compatibility of values or other attributes. One may therefore end up with a partner with whom one really has little in common.

☞ THE COLLECTION STORY

In the collection story, one's partner is chosen because of the way he or she fits into some overall collection, just as a coin, stamp, or baseball card might fit into a person's collection of these items. There is a certain detachment in the way a partner is viewed, much as an object in a collection is viewed with detachment. The partner may be seen as fitting perfectly into the individual's life but, as often as not, is only one element in the collection. The other elements may or may not be treated in the same way as the partner. Moreover, the partner may or may not be aware that these other elements exist.

Diagnosing the Collection Story

1   I like dating different partners simultaneously; each partner should fit a particular need.

2 I think it is okay to have multiple partners who fulfill my different needs.

3 I sometimes like to think about how many people I could potentially date all at the same time.

4 I believe love is like a collection of coins: the greater the variety, the more exciting the collection.

5 I don't believe any one partner can be all that I need. Therefore, I prefer to have multiple partners, each fulfilling different needs.

6 I enjoy having multiple intimate partners simultaneously, each with a unique place in my life.

7 I find it difficult to be happy when I have only one intimate partner.

8 I tend and like to have multiple intimate partners at once, each fulfilling a somewhat different role.

Ian and Jennifer

Everything is going pretty well for Ian. He has received straight A's for the third consecutive semester, he is captain of the basketball team, and his social life is more than acceptable. However, something seems to be missing. It is his senior year of college, and he doesn't have a steady girlfriend. Most of his friends are going out with someone, and although in the past he questioned these friends on how they could possibly manage being tied down to just one person, he now feels that it is time for him to do just that. Indeed, having a girlfriend would be the perfect complement to his life.

There is only one problem: Ian doesn't know whom to choose as his partner. Many women like him, and several of these women have already tried to get him to commit to a serious relationship, but he really doesn't like any one of them more than any of the rest. Nevertheless, he feels that some of the women would make worse partners than others. Kathy, for one, might become overly possessive, and Janet seems the dependent type; both would require too much of his time. Sarah, on the other hand, is usually busy with her music and hence would not always be there for him when he needed her. Pam has a great personality, but she isn't as pretty as

Ian would like. Both Amy and Jennifer seem independent, and neither is as busy as Sarah. In addition, they are both attractive and outgoing, so he would feel comfortable being seen with them in public. After pondering it for a moment, Ian decides that Jennifer would make the better partner of the two, because she is a senior and would therefore be able to accompany him to all of the senior activities throughout the year. Moreover, Jennifer is one of the women who tried to get him to commit to a more serious relationship in the past, so he figures the courtship process should not be that time-consuming.

Having made his decision, Ian calls Jennifer and asks her if she is still interested in making a commitment. Jennifer is a bit taken aback by his proposal. After all, Ian has never shown any genuine interest in her. It seems odd that he would want to jump right into a relationship. Nevertheless, she is flattered by his proposal, and agrees to start seeing him on a regular basis. Upon hanging up the phone, Ian feels quite satisfied, although hardly exuberant; Jennifer is simply the missing piece in his otherwise complete life.

The first few weeks of Ian's relationship with Jennifer are rather rough. There is no real intimacy between them, and they often have trouble finding things to talk about. Nevertheless, Ian likes the idea of having Jennifer as a girlfriend. Not only is she attractive and always there for him, but his friends are also consistently complimenting him on how lucky he is to have her. So whenever Jennifer mentions their lack of intimacy, Ian tries to convince her that things will change and that it is normal to have this sort of problem early in a relationship.

However, as time goes on, Ian wonders whether his life is really complete; perhaps there is still something missing. It isn't that he no longer wants Jennifer as his girlfriend; it's just that he misses some of the aspects of being unattached. At a recent party, he was flirting with someone from his biology class, and he had great difficulty turning down a request to walk her home. He knew what such a request entailed, and had Jennifer not been at the party, he would most likely have walked the woman home.

Martina and Chad

Arriving home from work, Martina walks quickly into the living room. With much anticipation, she asks her roommate, Sharon, if there were any calls for her. Sharon shakes her head in disbelief at this question. After all, on average, Martina receives about fifteen calls a day, and today has been no exception. For the most part, and at times almost exclusively, these calls are from men who want a date with her. Ordinarily this would not be that shocking, especially when you consider that Martina is a beautiful, outgoing young woman. However, she happens to have a boyfriend. What makes the situation more unusual is that Martina hands out her number to just about any attractive man who asks for it, even though she rarely intends to go out with any of them. She simply wants to have a long string of men interested in her. After all, she already has someone with whom she can go out all of the time. Indeed, Chad, her boyfriend, with his good looks and dynamic personality, fits that role perfectly.

Sharon is extremely perplexed by the way Martina treats the men in her life—especially Chad. It is quite obvious that Martina does not feel emotionally attached to Chad, and that she views him almost as an inanimate object that she can show around to all of her friends, rather than as a real person. Because of this fact, Sharon often asks her roommate why she sees only Chad when she has all of these other desirable and available men asking her out. Martina responds that it is nice to have one partner she can always count on to be there for her; moreover, she feels that seeing more than one man would simply be too time-consuming. Sharon then asks Martina why she gives all of these other men her number; after all, if her only purpose is to gain the attention of lots of attractive guys, isn't it enough that they eagerly ask for her number? Martina sees her roommate's point but maintains that she likes to have them calling her; that way, in case something goes wrong with her relationship with Chad, she will have several men to choose from, any of whom would fit the role of boyfriend just as well as Chad does. Sharon remains bewildered by the way Martina handles her relationship with Chad.

After returning all of her phone calls, Martina changes her clothes and gets ready for her dinner date with Chad. Chad is already waiting for Martina at the restaurant when she arrives, which is the way she usually plans it, because it makes her look better to have him waiting for her rather than the other way around. She gives Chad a pleasant though quite formal kiss on his cheek. As she looks at him closely, she notices that his lower lip is a bit swollen. When she brings it up, he tells her that it had somehow gotten infected and that he needed to have minor surgery done on it. Martina does not even ask him if he is all right, or if the surgery was painful; rather, she just wants to know how long his lip is going to look gross. She is relieved when he tells her that everything should be back to normal in a couple of days. After all, she always wants Chad to look his best.

Modes of Thought and Behavior

In a collection story, partners (usually there are more than one) are viewed as fitting into some overall scheme, much as pieces of art, coins, stamps, or baseball cards might fit into a collection. The partner or partners are often considered in a somewhat detached way, precisely because they have many of the characteristics of objects in a collection.

Of the various stories considered in this book, the collection story is the most explicitly polygamous. It is rare for someone having this story to be satisfied with only one relationship, much as it would be rare for a collector to have just a single piece of art, or a single coin, in his or her collection. The relationships may all differ somewhat from each other, and indeed are likely to, much as elements of a collection are more interesting if they differ from each other in certain ways. Thus, one person may primarily fulfill a need for intimacy, another a need for passion, and so on. Collectors may find that their best friend is not their lover, is not the individual they most admire, and is not their favorite person with whom to spend time.

Collectors like Ian or Martina are likely to find that as soon as they decide to commit to a relationship, they feel a sense of reactance; that is, they feel as though their freedom is being encroached upon.[1] They may even feel trapped. The result is that they may decide to cut short the commitment, or they may devise strategies, such as seeing other people, that allow them to continue to partake of their collection mentality.

Complementary Roles: Collector and Collectible

The two complementary roles in the collection story are the collector and the collectible, so to speak. One person is collected by the other. Typically, though, there will be multiple persons in the collection, so that there are multiple collectibles. It is also possible for both individuals to be collectors, in which case they each function in both roles simultaneously, often without realizing this fact. For example, were Ian and Martina dating, they might each be busily fitting the other into a limited role, oblivious to the fact that they are receiving pretty much the same thing they are giving.

The collector tends to have a certain detachment from his or her partner, who is, after all, an object in a collection. Thus, this individual is likely to show what is sometimes referred to as an *avoidant attachment style:* The individual prefers to maintain emotional distance from partners.[2]

Advantages and Disadvantages

There are a few possible advantages to a collection story. For one thing, the collector generally cares about the collectible's physical well-being, as appearance is much of what makes a collection shine. The collector also finds a way of meeting multiple needs. Usually these needs will be met in parallel—by having several intimate relationships at the same time—but a collector may also enter into serial monogamous relationships, where each successive relationship meets a need or set of needs that the last relationship did not meet.

In a society that values monogamy, collection stories work best if they do not become serious or if individuals in the collection beyond the main partner are viewed as clearly and qualitatively different in terms of the needs they meet, such as friendship or intellectual stimulation.

The disadvantages of the collection story become most obvious when people are trying to form serious relationships and to go beyond dating multiple partners. The collector may find it difficult to establish intimacy, or anything approaching a complete relationship involving intimacy with, passion for, and commitment toward a single individual. The collectible does not get the whole of the collector, and upon discovering this fact is likely to feel quite disturbed, unless the collectible is also a collector or prefers a less involved relationship. Collections can also become expensive, time-consuming, and in some cases illegal (as when an individual enters into multiple marriages simultaneously).

☞ THE ART STORY

In the art story, the individual views the partner as a work of art, dwelling on his or her overall physical appearance, or on aspects of it (such as the eyes, the physique, the torso, and so on). The admiration the individual feels for the partner in some ways resembles that felt toward a work of art that an individual considers virtually priceless.

Diagnosing the Art Story

1 One of the pleasures of life for me is being able to enjoy the physical beauty of my partner.
2 Physical attractiveness is quite honestly the most essential characteristic that I look for in a partner.
3 I usually do not even consider partners who are not physically quite attractive.
4 I enjoy being surrounded by beautiful things, especially a good-looking partner.
5 I would like to be able to watch and admire my partner, like a work of art.
6 I cannot imagine myself making a permanent commitment to someone who is not physically attractive.

7   It is very important to me that my partner always looks good.

8   Unusual physical attractiveness in a partner is very important to me.

Stan and Ellen

Stan has been in Bill's Sports Emporium for almost three minutes now, and Ellen has yet to take her eyes off him. He looks like a statue that has suddenly come to life after a thousand motionless years in a museum. His jaw is tightly chiseled, and his eyes are like two pieces of turquoise. With his broad shoulders and tall, powerful build, it seems perfectly logical that he should be in a sporting goods store. Ellen, who works at the store, walks up to him and, with a suggestive smile, asks if there is anything she can do for him. After he tells her that he is looking for a basketball, she takes him over to the appropriate location, mentioning along the way that she is a huge basketball fan (although she has never picked up a ball in her life). After selecting a ball, Stan tells her that he plays every Saturday at the YMCA and that she should come and watch, because there are always some pretty good games. She replies that she will be sure to be there, and, with another suggestive smile, she says that she will give him the 20 percent discount that she gives her friends.

As Stan leaves the store, Ellen turns to her coworker, Beth, who happened to overhear the entire conversation with Stan. Ellen can hardly contain her excitement, while Beth can only shake her head. Ellen is shocked to see Beth's reaction and asks if she has had her eyes checked recently. Beth admits that Stan is cute but wonders how Ellen could possibly have overlooked how stupid he is; in her opinion, there is no possible way that he could have made it past the sixth grade. Ellen acknowledges that intelligence is not Stan's strong suit, but what matters much more to her is physical attractiveness, and Stan has to be the most handsome man she has ever seen.

Saturday has arrived and Ellen is busy watching Stan play basketball. She loves to see him dribble the ball up and down the court, but she does not like to see him dash after a loose ball or go up for a rebound; after all, she does not want her perfect specimen damaged in any way. Fortunately, Stan finishes the game unscathed, and after washing up, he and Ellen go out to lunch.

Beth was right about Stan's intelligence; he seems to have trouble putting together anything but the simplest of sentences, and he has difficulty understanding any conversation that does not deal with basketball. Nevertheless, Ellen is able to look beyond all of Stan's intellectual shortcomings, as long as she can stare at his perfectly sculpted face.

Stan and Ellen have been seeing each other for four weeks now, but Beth is still in disbelief. As she and Ellen take inventory in the store, Beth continues to point out the obvious fact that Ellen will never be able to have a serious conversation with Stan and, beyond that, will never be able to love him for anything more than his appearance. Ellen does not deny this, but maintains that at this point in her life, all she wants is the most gorgeous guy she can find.

Steve and Alana

Steve cannot believe that he is already back at college. He knows that this past summer was longer than the ones he had had in high school, but it certainly did not seem that way. As he sits now in the first class of his sophomore year, all he can think about is the wonderful array of beautiful women who packed the beaches by his family's summer home. Steve's reveries, however, are soon interrupted when a gorgeous young blonde, with bright blue eyes and a perfect body, walks into the room. At first Steve thinks that he might still be lost in his daydreams. With her incredible looks and dark tan, she might very well have been one of the women he had drooled over during the summer. Fortunately, he is able to regain his composure when she sits down next to him, and, trying to capitalize on his opportunity, he casually initiates some small talk with her.

Her name is Alana, and this is her first year at college. Their conversation over the next few minutes is not exactly the most stimulating one, and Steve finds Alana to be a bit arrogant. Nevertheless, he is still enthralled by her looks; actually, he is convinced that she is the most beautiful woman in the entire school. And so, after class, he asks her if she would like to go to a movie with him. She accepts, and they make plans for the weekend.

Two months later, Steve's best friend, Tim, cannot believe that Steve is still seeing Alana. Tim feels that Alana has nothing going for her aside from her looks. He finds her snotty, selfish, and obnoxious. Steve disagrees with his friend, although he can see how Tim might feel this way about her; he argues, however, that Alana's first impression is deceiving, and that once you get to know her, she turns out to be a really great person. Tim does not think that Steve actually believes what he is saying; rather, he thinks that Steve is so physically attracted to Alana that he has blinded himself to her horrible personality. Steve does admit that Alana's looks are the main reason he is going out with her. However, he denies that her physical appeal has colored his overall opinion of her. Tim just shakes his head, warning Steve that when winter comes, Alana will lose her tan, and with all the extra time that she will be spending in the library rather than in the gym, she will start to put on some pounds as well. He adds that when this transformation occurs, Steve will see that Tim is correct in his belief. Although still holding his ground, Steve finds it almost painful to think of Alana without her dark tan and fabulous figure.

Modes of Thought and Behavior

In the art story, individuals tend to love their partners for their physical attractiveness. The individuals may not, and often do not, recognize this tendency in themselves. Indeed, they may see their partner's physical attractiveness as a nice bonus, but incidental to their feelings toward their partner. Or, as in the cases of Ellen and Steve, they may recognize their tendency to fall for attractive people, but justify it to their own satisfaction. When something happens to impair their partner's physical attractiveness, however, they may find that their feelings for the partner fade fast, and often right away. If

Stan has a basketball accident, for example, chances are good that Ellen will be gone pretty quickly.

Because we are taught that beauty is only skin deep, people may be extremely reluctant to attribute the dissolution of their feelings to the change in physical appearance, and so may attribute the change to something else, such as the realization that the partner's personality isn't what it had seemed to be.

Complementary Roles: Admirer and Work of Art

The two complementary roles in the art story are the admirer of the work of art and the work of art, so to speak. In the above stories, of course, the admirers are Ellen and Steve. The admirer seeks the most beautiful artwork he or she can find.

The principles of evolutionary psychology suggest that what men and women find to be attractive may not be the same. While individuals differ in what they find attractive, men are likely to be attracted to women younger than themselves, in whom beauty is a reflection of health and a measure of their ability to produce viable offspring. Women, on the other hand, are more likely to be attracted to men older than themselves, who will be better able to bestow resources on them and thereby take better care not only of them but of their progeny.[1]

But research by Judith Langlois and her colleagues suggests that there is a constant in what people find physically attractive. This constant is not exactly what people might expect. We often expect that the most attractive individual among a set of individuals will be someone who is quite unusual and perhaps rather exotic. The research of Langlois, in contrast, suggests that what we find most attractive is the exact average—literally, a prototype of physical features.[2] Langlois and her colleagues used computer analysis to show participants in a study various computer-generated faces that differed in terms of the number of original faces that were "averaged" in order to generate the computer-produced sketches. Langlois discovered that the greater the number of averaged faces an image represented, the larger the number of people who found that face attractive. In other words, attractiveness is a kind of golden mean of the faces we have seen. The pursuer of art will usually be looking for someone who looks like everyone else—but more so![3]

The object of art may or may not realize that he or she is such an object to the art connoisseur. Some people may be flattered to be appreciated for their physical appearance; others may find the idea of being valued for their looks to be offensive. Someone like Stan may believe he is being valued for his basketball skills rather than his looks. The fact is, though, that a society favors those who look good by the standards of that society, and so physically attractive people tend to be more successful in practically everything they undertake.[4] Whether we like it or not, physical attractiveness makes a big difference to outcomes in life.

Those who recognize that they are objects of art and accept it are likely to do everything in their power to retain their attractive physical appearance. Although relatively few people will confess to valuing physical appearance very highly, the financial health of the cosmetics industry—not to mention the plastic surgery business—suggests that people count physical appearance far more than they care to admit.

The same is true even in initial encounters. A study done by Mark Snyder and his colleagues found that when individuals were supposedly matched to partners via a computer program (but were actually matched at random), the only factor that reliably predicted whether the couple enjoyed their first date and wanted to date again was physical attractiveness![5]

Advantages and Disadvantages

A positive feature of the art story is that people in it—or at least the admirer—tend to feel great physical attraction in the relationships into which they enter. This feeling is hardly surprising, because for these individuals, intense physical attraction is much of what motivates the relationship in the first place.

Of course, with this attraction comes a great concern that the partner maintain his or her high level of physical attractiveness. This concern can be a double-edged sword. On the one hand, the individual is likely to support the partner's desire to continue to look attractive—often despite whatever it may cost. On the other hand, the interest in physical attractiveness can be at the expense of other kinds of interest, and can become a full-time preoccupation as people age.

An obvious danger in this kind of relationship is that one or the other partner will lose interest as the normal processes of aging rob the "work of art" of his or her physical beauty. Men, in particular, seem to be susceptible to trading in their works of art for newer ones. These trade-ins can be motivated by a number of forces, such as the desire to bolster self-esteem by showing oneself (and possibly others) one's ability to attract a younger mate. At the same time, the process can be unending. Take the aging man who is highly successful. He may find that the latest of a string of spouses is much younger than his previous wives and perhaps more motivated by his resources—he is, after all, filthy rich—than by the desire to be with a much older mate.

RELATIONSHIP AS OBJECT

In stories where the relationship is the object, the relationship serves as a means to attain an end that has little or, more often, nothing directly to do with the relationship. In a house and home story, the relationship serves as a means to acquire and develop a comfortable and attractive living environment. In a recovery story, the relationship is used to help someone recover from a trauma or other difficult experience. In a religion story, the relationship is used as a means to come closer to God, or it becomes itself the embodiment of the individuals' religious feelings. In a game story, the relationship serves as the vehicle for playing an often complex game, with a set of rules and, typically, a winner and a loser, although who wins and who loses can vary from one round to the next.

☞ THE HOUSE AND HOME STORY

In a house and home story, the home is the center of the relationship. People put a great deal of attention into the home and into its being in the very best condition possible. They are typically very proud of the home, and view it as a focal point in their lives. Sometimes the home, which starts out symbolizing the relationship, seems to become more important than the relationship itself.

Diagnosing the House and Home Story

1 An ideal relationship is like a well-tended home—beautiful, immaculate, well ordered, something to be proud of.
2 Our house is the "home base" for our relationship. It is where we start and where we finish.
3 The home in which a couple lives is like an extension of them and their relationship.
4 When I do things for our home, I feel like I am doing things for my close relationship.
5 The truth is that people who let their homes go often find their relationships soon follow.
6 You can tell a lot about the quality of a couple's relationship by looking at the home in which they live.
7 I feel as though the home we keep together is an important part of our relationship.
8 I sometimes find it hard to imagine our relationship without our home as our refuge.

Arnold and Betsy

If you drive along Amtach Road, the residence of Arnold and Betsy will stick out from all the rest. The grass in the front yard is a luscious green, cut perfectly. A beautiful array of flowers surrounds the grass on all sides, with not a weed infiltrating the glorious display of color. A gravel driveway runs alongside the yard, ending at a newly painted garage with recently washed windows and neatly organized tools inside. To the left is the house itself. With an authentic Spanish tile roof, white stucco walls, and an antique door, it is no wonder that some people from a magazine that spotlights beautiful houses once asked if they could come in to see if the inside was as beautiful as the outside. As they walked around, their eyes were treated to a spotless home filled with handmade furniture, wonderful paintings, and an adorable little fireplace. They immediately asked if they could take pictures of the entire residence and put them in their magazine.

Arnold and Betsy have been married for thirty-six years. Arnold is responsible for most of the upkeep of the residence, especially the garden and the garage. Betsy sees to it that the house is kept clean and neat on the inside, but it is Arnold who usually decides what to buy, where it should go, and how often everything needs to be cleaned. At the moment, Arnold is busy with the front yard—mowing the lawn, watering the flowers, and taking special care that there are no weeds around. The front yard is Arnold's self-proclaimed pride and joy. He spends two hours a day—more on weekends—making sure that all is in working order. He knows that one missed day can lead to disaster, and that is something he definitely wants to avoid.

Arnold and Betsy's relationship has always been centered around the home. They believe that leading a healthy, productive life begins with a comfortable living environment. The excellent physical condition and overall success of the entire family are testimony to the workability of this belief for them. To an extent, the effort spent on keeping the house and garden in such perfect condition has taken away from the relationship between Betsy and Arnold. At times, it seems that every spare minute they have is spent taking care of the home, leaving very little time for them to spend with one another. Betsy had always imagined that things would be different after the children left. When their two daughters were around, most of Betsy and Arnold's time was spent in taking care of them; providing a clean, safe home was part of that care. After the girls grew up, Betsy thought, it would no longer be necessary to have such a high standard of perfection—not to mention the fact that, without the kids there to help them, it would be almost impossible to maintain the same level of upkeep. It seemed only natural that they should reduce the amount of effort that they put into the home; at the very least, they could cut down on all of the unnecessary, decorative aspects of their work. However, Arnold was determined to continue to shoot for the same level of perfection. To this day, Betsy tries to tell him that he should not get so worked up about it, but he refuses to listen to her. She does not blame him, of course; she knows that a thirty-year habit is hard to break. Moreover, it is not as though her husband is working on someone else's home; it is their home—the home that they have shared for more than half of their lives.

Sandi and Jack

For the first time in their lives, the children are playing basketball in their own driveway. Their father, Jack, recently installed a basket and a backboard above the garage. It took him a long time to do so, because he wanted to make sure not only that the rim was even, but that it was regulation height as well. After all, both he and his wife, Sandi, felt that the new basketball setup should be as perfect as the rest of their home. Speaking of the rest of their home, Sandi and Jack are busy seeing to it that everything is truly up to their high standards. Sandi is in the backyard, working carefully on her flower garden and on her fruit trees, while Jack is in the house constructing a bookcase that the whole family will be able to use. They have both been at it for several hours, but neither of them is showing any signs of fatigue or displeasure; in fact, they both seem to be enjoying what they are doing.

Jack and Sandi's children have now been playing basketball for an hour, and their mother has just come from the backyard to tell them that they need to start doing their chores before it gets too late. They must first rake the leaves in both the front and back yards, and then they must mow the entire lawn. At first the kids make a bit of a fuss, but they know how important a well-kept lawn is to their mother, and so they put the ball away and get ready to do their chores. The children also understand that they cannot put out a halfhearted effort and expect to get away with it; hence, as always, they will be careful not to leave even one leaf behind, and will make certain that the lawn is evenly cut.

After finishing her work in the backyard, Sandi goes inside and begins waxing all of the wooden furniture. Jack has just completed his task of making the bookcase, and after Sandi's approval, he sits down on the couch to relax for a minute. He shakes his head in amazement as he watches his wife tirelessly tend to her household duties. There was a time when Jack felt that Sandi spent too many hours a day working on their home, and that the effort she was putting into all of this work was taking something away from their relationship. Indeed, by the time all of the day's work is finished, there is precious little time that remains for them to do anything else. For a while, in fact, Jack thought that the maintenance of their beautiful home had become more important than their relationship. On many occasions he tried to persuade his wife that they should spend less time trying to make their home perfect and more time trying to make their relationship perfect.

Jack has since altered his view on Sandi's persistent dedication to their home. His turnabout came after one of his wife's replies to his concern that she was devoting too much time to their home at the expense of their time together. She first asked if there was anything really wrong with their relationship; although he tried to come up with something, Jack could not think of anything significant. She then asked if there was anything wrong with wanting to have a comfortable living environment; Jack replied that there was not, and was beginning to see that his complaints were losing some of their strength. Sandi concluded by remarking that they spend more time in their home than anywhere else, and that therefore the home can be seen as both the center of their lives and of their relationship. Hence, they should do their best to make it as perfect as possible. Jack was more or less persuaded by his wife's arguments, and ever since, he has spent as much time caring for their home as she has. At the same time, he worries that caring for the home could become a substitute for caring for each other if they are not careful.

Modes of Thought and Behavior

People with a house and home story view the home as the physical center of their relationship, and sometimes the emotional center as well. They are likely to put a substantial investment of resources into the home, both financially and in terms of their time and even emotional commitment. They may be constantly redoing their home, or adding things to it, or trading up to better homes, or even finding themselves competing with others they know so that they will have the very best home they can possibly have.

In the house and home story, the home becomes something more than just a place to live. It serves as a focal point to channel attention and even affection that may somehow have gotten displaced from the relationship. The couple, unable to shower attention on each other for whatever reason, displace it to the home, which is part of them.

Displacements of this kind really do not have to be limited to a house and home. They can be to a pet, children, a boat, a car, or any other tangible aspect of people's lives. Obviously, there is a fine line between just loving your home and displacing love from your partner to the home. The question is whether it is the home (boat, car, or whatever) that is receiving more attention, or the partner.

People with a house and home story may be quite happy with that story, of course. Perhaps the relationship isn't all that they had hoped for; if so, the home may provide the center or satisfaction that the relationship cannot provide without the home. Or perhaps the individual with this story has trouble showing affection toward other people. Or perhaps the individual is just genuinely concerned with a comfortable living environment, and thus devotes the attention to having one, attention that others would devote to other things.

Complementary Roles: Caretaker and Care Recipient

The complementary roles in the house and home story are either two caretakers (of the home), or the caretaker and the person who lives with the caretaker but is not the primary recipient of that person's attention and care. In the latter case, the person who lives with the caretaker is usually not asked to put in much time keeping up the home; the caretaker might not even want anyone else to "mess with" the home.

House and home stories probably work most smoothly when both individuals are in caretaker roles, so that they have the same focus of attention. When only one of them is, the danger is that the other will feel left out. Again, the particular object that gives the feeling of centeredness need not necessarily be the home—it might be a pet or a classic car or a coin collection. It is always tangible, however, and always seems to receive more attention than the partner.

Advantages and Disadvantages

The advantage of the house and home story is the explicit recognition that a comfortable living environment really can make a difference in a relationship. Research has shown that people tend to feel positively toward others when they have positive experiences in the presence of those others.[1] Thus, if individuals feel good about their home, these positive feelings may well spread to the relationship and to each other.

Moreover, a comfortable living environment also tends to produce less stress than an uncomfortable one. People who experience stress in their lives can inadvertently end up carrying over that stress into their relationship. For people with a house and home relationship, the home is typically a source of comfort rather than of stress, unless they become so obsessed with the home that they become unable ever to be at peace with the condition of the home, and start to feel stress over its never being perfect.

The potential disadvantages to this story are probably by now obvious. Attention can be diverted from the partner and the relationship to the home or other object. Arnold, for example, seems close to the point of obsession with the home, a source of some concern for his wife, Betsy. Jack, although he has accepted Sandi's preoccupation with the home, is afraid of where this preoccupation may be leading them. The relationship may suffer as the home improves. Eventually, the home actually may become more important than the relationship. In a society that promotes the great importance of material things, people may actually need to be on guard against losing their relationship as their focus shifts more and more toward the acquisition of material comforts.

☞ THE RECOVERY STORY

The recovery story is one of survival. The individual has been through some kind of trauma—substance abuse, victimization, prison, war, or other forms of violence—and seeks recovery through a relationship. Abraham Maslow spoke of deficiency love.[1] The goal of deficiency love is to find in another person something that one was never able to find in oneself. The metaphor of deficiency is particularly appropriate here, because the person seeking recovery hopes, somehow, that the other person will be able to bring about a recovery that one was never able to bring about oneself. Of course, it is very difficult, and often impossible, for someone else to give you what you cannot find in yourself.

In this story, both the person attempting to recover and the co-dependent, as the partner is sometimes called, become dependent on the past for their relationship. Their relationship feeds on putting the past behind them at the same time that this past is a vital part of the relationship. Ironically, the relationship may actually cease to function should the person in need of recovery actually recover. Upon recovery, the relationship may well have lost the reason for which it came into being and the motivation that resulted in its continuation.

Diagnosing the Recovery Story

CODEPENDENT

1 I often end up with people who face a specific problem in their past or present life, and I find myself helping them get their life back in order.
2 I enjoy being involved in relationships in which my partner needs my help to get over some problem.
3 I think a truly good relationship could mean the beginning of a new life for those individuals who have had to face unfortunate circumstances in their lives.
4 I often find myself with partners who need my help to recover from the hurts of their past.

PERSON IN RECOVERY

1 I need someone who will help me recover from my painful past.
2 I believe that a relationship can save me from a life that is crumbling around me.
3 I need help getting over my past.
4 The best relationship would be one in which my partner and I both could devote a great deal of time and effort helping me to get over my past.

Jacob and Alice

Jacob is lucky to be alive. Six weeks ago, after drinking twelve beers at a local bar, he drove his car headfirst into a tree. He was in a coma for thirty-six hours, and the doctors initially believed he would never come out of it. When Jacob finally regained consciousness, he realized that he had to do something about his life.

Despite encouragement from his friends, Jacob had never sought help for his alcohol problem; even though it had cost him his job and his girlfriend, he always thought that he had it under control. However, following the accident, he knew he could not put off treatment any longer. Only hours after being released from the hospital, Jacob attended his first AA meeting.

Jacob has been sober ever since the accident, and tonight he is going on his first date since his girlfriend left him. It was not an easy decision for Jacob to ask Alice out; he recalls very well that whenever a problem arose in his last relationship, he would turn to alcohol as a solution. Of course, this is only his first date with Alice, but he senses a strong bond between them and believes that this date will evolve into something more substantial.

Jacob also knows, however, that no matter how well things might go for him and Alice, he will still have to face many of the same problems that drove him to alcohol in the past. Nevertheless, Jacob is confident that things will be different this time. He believes that his failed relationships and his near-fatal car accident have given him a new perspective on alcohol that will prevent him from his ever using it again as a solution to his problems. He also feels the advice he received in the AA meetings will help keep him from abusing alcohol when the desire to do so arises. Finally, he believes that Alice, too, will help him recover from his past problems. She seems both compassionate and considerate—the type of person who not only will be understanding of his predicament, but also will be able to help him through the tough periods that he most likely will have to face.

Jacob takes Alice to a small Italian restaurant that was strongly recommended to him by a friend. Neither Jacob nor his friend took into consideration the fact that, for many people, it is customary to have a bottle of wine for dinner at an Italian restaurant. As a result, when Alice asks Jacob for his wine preference, he does not know how to respond. He had intended on waiting awhile before bringing up his history with alcohol, but he now realizes that he must tell Alice about it right away.

After listening to his story, Alice tells Jacob that she appreciates his honesty and that she is still willing to see him, despite his past. Jacob is quite relieved, and he assures her that he knows starting up a new relationship will be difficult for him, and he will do his best to confront all of the challenges it presents without resorting to alcohol. Jacob speaks with a conviction that he is not sure he truly has. Ironically, the tension of talking about his awful past experiences with alcohol makes him want it once again. For Jacob, it's one day at a time.

Leslie and Barry

Leslie believes that she is ready to put her troubled past behind her. She is only twenty-one, yet she has suffered enough for an entire lifetime. When she was a child, her father physically and sexually abused her, causing her to run away from home when she was just fifteen years old. She hitchhiked across the country until her food money ran out.

Leslie looked for work, but there was not much demand for an unskilled high-school dropout. As is often the case in this type of situation, Leslie came into contact with the wrong crowd, in the form of Billy, a smooth-talking local. After some alluring promises and misguided information, Leslie found herself working in a seedy strip joint. She was ashamed and disgusted by what she was doing, but she realized that she had to do something to earn money for food and shelter. To make matters worse, her obvious anxiety and insecurity made it difficult for her to perform at the club. In order to make it easier for her, Billy gave her some amphetamines to eliminate her inhibitions. After a few months, even though she no longer needed the amphetamines to perform, she had become addicted to them. This drug addiction, along with the abusive relationship that she had unwillingly formed with Billy, made Leslie's life all but unbearable.

Almost unbelievably, Leslie survived this lifestyle for six years, and after saving enough money behind Billy's back, she managed to get out of the city in which life had been sheer torture for her. She took a bus across the country and almost immediately began working as a waitress. Anne, a coworker, told Leslie that Leslie could stay at her place until she found a place of her own.

While living at Anne's, Leslie was introduced to Anne's brother, Barry, and immediately they fell for each other. Leslie knew that she would have to tell Barry about her past, and she did so the first time she had an opportunity. Surprisingly, he took it very well and wanted to go out with her anyway. In fact, he was quite impressed with her perseverance and her willingness to start a relationship, considering all that she had been through. He understood, however, that this troubled past would make it very difficult for her to become intimate with anyone. Moreover, he knew that because of her prior addiction, Leslie might very well turn to drugs if she were to fall upon hard times. Barry also realized that he might merely be a transitional figure for Leslie. For the first time in her life she was living peacefully, and it was possible that she needed him simply to help her get her bearings straight before moving on. Despite all of these potential problems, however, Barry was optimistic that things would go well.

Leslie and Barry have now been seeing each other for several months, and Barry appears to have been correct in his optimistic prediction. Anne often jokes with Leslie about some of Barry's idiosyncrasies, such as his odd sleeping position, which would be worthy of an acrobat. Leslie just shakes her head, explaining that, after what she has had to deal with in the past, almost anything is tolerable, especially a harmless habit. She adds that Barry has been instrumental in her recovery.

In recent months, Leslie has had many horrifying nightmares and flashbacks from her past, and Barry has always come to her side and comforted her in these situations. Without him, Leslie believes that she might have resorted to drugs to get through these tough periods. In addition to this support, Barry has been considerate of the fact that this is Leslie's first truly intimate relationship, and he has agreed to take things very slowly with it.

Leslie isn't sure whether the relationship with Barry will last. The whole thing seems almost too good to be true. But right now, Leslie needs Barry more, she feels, than anything, and she is glad to have him with her.

Modes of Thought and Behavior

The recovery story is a risky one for both partners. The characteristic mode of thinking for the person in recovery is that he or she has survived something—drugs, alcohol, disastrous relationships, trauma of some kind—and is ready to move on. But this desire for recovery can hide some difficulties.

One potential problem is that sometimes the person wants to recover but may not actually succeed. He or she wants to stop using alcohol, but doesn't have the courage to do so; or the person wants to stop drug use but isn't really quite ready to go through the pain of stopping. The person who chooses a role as codependent is often someone who believes that he or she can pull the other person out of the pits. But as in the case of any addiction, only the addicted person can decide to end the addiction. The codependent is thus liable to get sucked into an unending recovery story that never actually leads to any real recovery, but only to an imagined process of recovery.

A second risk in such relationships is that the recovery will be extremely painful for both parties and tear the relationship apart. People coming out of awful relationships, or out of drug or alcohol dependencies, are often not at their best. A relationship with someone that might work at another time might not work when the person is going through recovery.

A third risk—mentioned earlier—is that if the person does actually recover, the role of the codependent will no longer make sense. The person may not be able to shift roles or may enjoy only the codependent role. Alternatively, the person who has made it through recovery may not wish to be with the codependent anymore, finding him or her irrelevant or a reminder of a painful past.

The fourth and perhaps greatest risk is that the relationship will be built on a foundation of illness rather than health. If recovery becomes the central focus of the relationship, the previous addiction may represent the foundation of the relationship, rather than an unpleasant stage of life that someone needs to put behind him or her.

Complementary Roles: Recoverer and Codependent

The most typical roles in the recovery story are the individual who is recovering and the codependent, whose role it is to help the individual to recover. It is important to realize that both partners can be dependent on each other, not just the recovering individual on the codependent. The codependent may equally need to feel that he or she is helping the person in recovery, just as the person in recovery needs to feel that he or she is being helped.

Another pairing of roles in a recovery story is one of two people who are recovering together, with each serving simultaneously as persons undergoing recovery and as codependents for each other. Both may be recovering from bad relationships, from drugs, or whatever. Such relationships are especially challenging, because both individuals are at such vulnerable points in their lives and typically are so needy that they cannot fully serve as codependents for each other. These relationships are likely to be at risk unless the individuals, at the time they meet, are quite far along in the recovery process. In this case, they can feel that they have something in common that few other people share, and this feeling of sharing can give them a special bond that many others do not enjoy.

Advantages and Disadvantages

The main advantage to a recovery story is that the codependent may really help the other partner to recover, so long as the other partner has genuinely made the decision to recover. Many of us know individuals who sought to reform their partners, only to experience total frustration when their partners made little or no effort to reform. At the same time, the codependent is someone who needs to feel he or she is helping someone, and gains this feeling of making a difference to someone through the relationship.

The main disadvantages in recovery relationships are the risk factors already described. Ultimately, others can assist in recovery, but the decision to recover, and the pain that recovery entails, must be borne by the person in need of recovery. As a result, recovery stories can assist in, but not produce, recovery in an individual.

THE RELIGION STORY

Here I refer to two kinds of religion stories. However, the two kinds can also be viewed as two different stories.

In one kind of religion story, religion is an integral part of the story of a loving relationship. The partners in the relationship typically see themselves not only in partnership with each other, but in partnership with God, by whose grace their relationship started and continues. In theory, and occasionally in practice, the religion need not even involve any kind of deity, although for our purposes here, we will refer to religion stories as involving God in some role.

The role God or another deity plays may vary as a function of the religion. Most typically, God is seen as infusing the entire relationship. Thus, God is not some third partner, but rather an integral part of every aspect of the relationship. Without God there would be no relationship. God may also be viewed as a third (perhaps higher-order) partner. Or God may be viewed more abstractly, as providing guidance in the way the relationship and its interface with the world should proceed.

In the second kind of religion story, the religion, in effect, is the relationship. The individual seeks salvation through the relationship. Thus, the person hopes the relationship will supply what religion typically has not. A partner may see his or her lover in much the way someone else would see a religious figure—as the partner's source of salvation.

Diagnosing the Religion Story

RELIGION IN RELATIONSHIP

1 I cannot imagine myself in a relationship in which my partner does not share my spiritual beliefs.

2 I believe that the closeness and unity involved in a close relationship almost require that partners have similar religious beliefs.

3 My devotion to my partner can only be seen in the larger context of my devotion to God.

4 The love that I feel for my partner has a sacred place within my heart, just as my spiritual beliefs do.

5 I believe true love should be a part of, rather than separate from, one's religious life.

6 I believe love is like spiritual belief in that it can be truly recognized only by your heart, rather than by your mind.

7 I believe that in the best relationships, people help each other draw closer to God.

8 It is very important to me that my partner share my religious beliefs.

RELATIONSHIP AS RELIGION

1 I seem to seek salvation in relationships, much as other people do in religion.

2 I feel like my relationship has saved me from despair.

3 Relationships can serve much the same function for me that religion does for other people.

4 I don't know what I would do without my partner.

5 My relationship has saved me from myself.

6 I have found that I need religion less now that I am in the relationship I'm in.

7 When I do not feel really involved in a relationship, I feel as though I am lost at sea.

8 To me, having a relationship is like having a religion.

Jerry and Ruby

Sitting quietly in his room, Jerry listens with sadness to the loud argument that his parents are having down the hall. He cannot hear what they are saying, but it does not matter; the only important thing is that, over the years, their love for one another has dwindled to a remnant of what it once must have been. Jerry hopes that the love he shares with his girlfriend, Ruby, will never disintegrate the way his parents' love has, and that they will always be as close as they are now.

So far Jerry and Ruby's relationship has lasted six months, and throughout that time they have been virtually inseparable. For them, love is more powerful than anything else in the world.

Whenever Jerry has a problem, he looks to Ruby to help him get through it. He believes that her compassion and her wisdom, as well as her strong love for him, will help him surmount all of the obstacles that life puts in his way. In accordance with this belief, Jerry is just now wiping away his tears and getting ready to go over to Ruby's house; he is certain that her company will help him cope with the hard times he is having at home.

Jerry slips out of the house, easily avoiding his parents, who are too busy screaming at each other to notice his departure. He drives over to Ruby's house and enters through the back door—always kept open in case of a late-night occasion such as this one. He walks upstairs to Ruby's room, being careful not to wake her mother. He tiptoes to the side of her bed and gently shakes her shoulder. As she gets up, she notices his tears and gives him a warm hug. They lie down and discuss the situation, holding each other closely the entire time. Jerry makes Ruby promise him that they will never go through the turmoil that has defined the relationship between his parents. Ruby assures him of this, easing his pain by telling him how much she loves him. She adds that nothing will ever get in the way of the love that they share. She explains that the feelings they have for each other are stronger than anything else in the world—so strong they practically can be etched in stone.

While listening to Ruby's words, Jerry nods in agreement, smiling peacefully as he does so. There are no longer any tears on his face. Once again Ruby has been able to get Jerry through a difficult moment in his life by assuring him of how powerful and unwavering their love for one another will always be. With this on his mind, Jerry closes his eyes and falls asleep in Ruby's arms.

Brenda and Timothy

Along with three hundred others, Brenda went to the main lawn at Mayberry College to hear a fellow student, Timothy, give a speech on the importance of God. Brenda listened attentively as Timothy expressed his view that we must all fight the horror of the world, as well as the evil urges dwelling inside of us, by looking to God and the unconditional love that he has for humankind. Timothy argued that we must follow God's example by loving others as he loves us.

Brenda, like many of those around her, was strongly influenced by Timothy's words. Her emotional involvement, however, was perhaps stronger than anyone else's, because of the recent event that almost took her life. She was riding her bike across the campus late one night when she approached an intersection by the gym. Ordinarily there are almost no cars that pass through this intersection at night, and Brenda had grown accustomed to riding straight through it. On this night, however, there was a car at the intersection, and it was moving at a fairly high speed. Miraculously, Brenda was able to slam on the brakes of her bike in time to narrowly avert an accident. Even though Brenda was not hurt, the incident was traumatic for her. It caused her to contemplate her place in the world more thoroughly than she had ever done before; as she did so, she started to feel as though everything she was doing was wrong and, moreover, that there was something missing in her life. As she listened to Timothy's words on God and love, she almost felt as though he were addressing her directly.

At the end of the speech, Brenda wished to talk to Timothy about what he said. She walked up to where he was standing and told him how much his words meant to her. She asked him if there was any way that the two of them could sit down at some point and talk about his ideas in more detail. Timothy was flattered by Brenda's praise and invited her to come over to his house.

That night Brenda and Timothy spent several hours talking about the latter's views on God and love. They discussed Brenda's near-fatal accident and the soul searching to which it led. Timothy listened closely to Brenda's concerns about her life and tried to help her out as best he could. He told her of similar situations in his own life and of how he was able to confront them by turning to God. They talked well into the night, and would have talked longer, but Brenda finally had to tell Timothy with regret that she had to leave. Before she left, however, they arranged to meet again.

Six weeks have passed since Brenda's first conversation with Timothy, and over that time they have been practically inseparable. Brenda regards her relationship with Timothy as the most important thing in the world to her. She credits him with turning her life around, and she hopes that the love they share, through the grace of God, will never die.

Modes of Thought and Behavior

The religion story either views love as serving the function of a religion (as in the case of Jerry and Ruby) or views religion as an integral part of love (as in the case of Brenda and Timothy). In either case, religion is a critical part of the relationship. Its part is quite different in the two kinds of religion stories, however.

In one case, love is salvation, which is how psychologist Theodore Reik suggested we see love.[1] We seek through another person the salvation we cannot find in any other way. In the other case, only religion can bring salvation, but love of another person can help make one's life much richer, and also help one fulfill one's responsibilities toward God.

Complementary Roles: Coreligionists, Savior and Salvation Seeker

There are a number of possible complementary roles in a religion story. One set of such roles involves two individuals who have a loyalty to each other and to their religion. They are coreligionists who participate in their religion individually and collectively. Timothy and Brenda fall into this set of roles. A second possible set of roles is savior and the person seeking salvation, as in the case of Jerry's seeking salvation through Ruby. In this second case, it is also possible for each member of a couple to seek salvation through the other, so that each individual is simultaneously the person seeking salvation and the savior.

Advantages and Disadvantages

Most religions of the world have encouraged marriage, which is a source of stability (and, incidentally, of future members of the religion). The religion story in which two people view themselves in a relationship infused with the presence of God generally seems to be an adaptive one, and churches that encourage this point of view seem to have relatively low divorce rates among their members. Of course, these lower divorce rates reflect not just happiness of the relationship but also the tendency of such religions, at least as they are practiced, to discourage divorce.

Viewing love as a source of salvation—the other kind of religion story—is risky, for much the same reason that love as a source of recovery is risky. For one thing, salvation probably cannot come successfully from another person. As a result, those who look to relationships for salvation are likely to be disappointed. Moreover, those who seek salvation through relationships usually are themselves in a sufficiently desperate state that, although they may be fully ready to receive love, they may not be ready fully to give it.

THE GAME STORY

The game story goes back at least to Ovid, who described love as ludic, or gamelike.[1] This view of love is also captured in John Lee's notion of the gamelike, or ludic, lover.[2]

What distinguishes the game story from other gamelike stories or stories about love being fun is that in this story the game is what is called "zero-sum": There is a winner and a loser, and as one individual comes closer to winning, the other comes closer to losing.[3] Thus, the game story involves a kind of competition, although one of the partners may be unaware that the competition is taking place. Often, multiple individuals are involved in the game, but only one partner may be aware of this fact, or both partners may be aware, but with respect to different players. They may both be playing the same game without either partner realizing it.

One of the most well-known expressions of the game story in film can be found in the movie *Who's Afraid of Virginia Woolf?* where Richard Burton and Elizabeth Taylor have constructed an elaborate game in which each is continually trying to undercut the other. But each is also dependent on the other to play the game and to follow the rules. When the rules change, it spells disaster for the relationship. Burton and Taylor suck another young couple into their game, destroying that couple along with themselves.

Games do not have to be as destructive as the Taylor-Burton game, but their competitive nature is at odds with the way we typically define close relationships. Judson Mills and Margaret Clark have distinguished between communal relationships—in which there is a give-and-take where no "records" are kept—and exchange relationships, in which there is a fairly careful tit-for-tat, with both partners in the relationship keeping track of who is giving and receiving what.[4] Game stories are about exchange, not communal relationships.

Diagnosing the Game Story

1   I believe love is like a game; sometimes you win, sometimes you lose.
2   I believe dating is much like a game; you play your part and hope to win.
3   I like to look at relationships as a game; my loss may be somebody else's gain, and vice versa.
4   I view my relationships as games. The uncertainty of winning or losing is part of the excitement of the game.
5   I believe partners in a relationship are like opponents in a game; each side aims at minimizing losses and maximizing gains.
6   When a romantic partner breaks up with me, I feel like I have lost in a game.
7   When I am with a partner in a relationship, I find myself thinking in terms of who is winning and who is losing.
8   I believe relationships are a game much like any other.

Jill and Stephen

Jill and Stephen belong to the same health club. Occasionally they glance flirtatiously at each other, but they have yet to exchange a word. Today, however, Stephen notices that Jill has left her gym bag in the weight room, and, seizing the opportunity, he picks it up and chases after her. Jill acts surprised and grateful when he hands her the bag, although she had intended to leave it behind, knowing that Stephen had been eyeing her and would almost certainly see that she had left it.

They have a light conversation, and it is obvious from the outset that neither wants to sound too interested in the other. As an aside, Jill mentions how much fun she's been having in the yoga class that the health club offers. Stephen responds by telling her that he has always considered going to one of these classes (which, of course, he hasn't really considered) but that he has never gotten around to it. Jill tells him that a class is starting up in five minutes and that he should come along. He readily agrees, although he is careful not to seem too excited.

After the class ends, Stephen casually asks Jill for her phone number. She gives it to him, and they go their separate ways. That night Stephen sits by the phone, wondering whether to call Jill. He decides it would be best to wait a day, just to keep her guessing. When he finally calls her, she tells him that she is busy and that she'll call him back when she gets a chance. In reality, Jill isn't busy at all, but she doesn't want Stephen to think that she's just sitting by the phone, waiting for him to call.

Eventually Stephen and Jill start spending time with one another; however, just as it was in the health club and on the phone, each of them treats the other as a friendly competitor in a game, rather than as a partner in a budding relationship. It is as if they both want to feel that they are somehow winning the game at the expense of the other. For instance, Jill always tries to make it seem as though Stephen wants her more than she wants him. She waits for him to make a sexual pass at her; then, even though she wants to reciprocate his movements, she backs off, teasing him with a sly laugh.

Stephen, the more competitive of the two, turns everything into a literal contest. While hanging out at a bar the other night, he set up a game whereby the winner would be the one who was approached by the largest number of people. He and Jill separated themselves by a distance long enough to ensure that others would not think they were together, yet short enough to be able to keep tabs on one another. At first this little contest was quite exciting; at the very least it was a change of pace from the standard bar outing. However, when they decided to tally up the score, there was a minor discrepancy between the number of people that Stephen believed had approached him, and the number Jill had observed approaching him.

Jill eventually wanted to drop the subject, but Stephen continued to insist that he was right.

For the most part, Stephen and Jill enjoy the little games in their relationship. Without these games, their time together wouldn't be as enjoyable. Both regard the games as fun and exciting. Stephen likes it when Jill teases him. He finds that it makes him even more attracted to her. And Jill likes all the contests that Stephen sets up for them. She not only enjoys it when she beats him; she also derives pleasure from watching him gloat after he wins.

Occasionally, however, Jill and Stephen's competitiveness gets in the way of their becoming more intimate. Stephen will not be completely open with Jill about his innermost feelings, because he fears that she will regard such an act as a sign that he wants her more than she wants him, and that she will then move on to someone else whom she sees as being harder to get. Jill, too, will not be completely open with Stephen, because she senses this dilemma of his, and doesn't want to relinquish what she considers to be an aspect of the relationship in which she feels she is winning.

Wes and Gina

Wes thought that Gina would give him at least one point. They have been playing racquetball for almost forty-five minutes, and Wes is getting dizzy from futilely trying to catch up with the little blue ball that has been bouncing off just about everything in the court except his paddle. Gina is relentless in her attempt to keep him from scoring any points. Finally he hits a good shot, but instead of congratulating him, she contends that he hit her previous shot on the second bounce and therefore should lose the point. Wes is convinced that he hit the shot on the first bounce, but at the moment he thinks that whether or not he did is completely irrelevant. After all, he just made his first good shot of the day; she should be happy for him. Wes gets upset and walks off the court. He gathers his things and goes out to Gina's car, where he sits on the hood and waits for her to come out and apologize.

Wes and Gina have been going out for six months, and there are times when Wes thinks that Gina sees the two of them as being involved in a competition rather than a relationship. She is determined to be the best at everything—not just at racquetball and other naturally competitive ventures, but at things as seemingly uncompetitive as taking down phone messages. Wes sees Gina as someone who could turn this seemingly mindless task into a challenge of who can take down the better, more comprehensive messages.

Gina also turns the romantic aspects of their relationship into a competition. One of her favorite things to do is to play a kissing game with Wes; the two of them sit so that there are just a few inches between their lips, and the winner is the one who resists the temptation to kiss the other the longest. Gina has never lost this game, as Wes always succumbs to his desire to kiss her; after all, he knows that if he does not kiss her, they will sit there all day, because Gina would never give Wes the satisfaction of winning.

For the most part, Wes does not mind Gina's competitiveness. It turns a lot of seemingly unexciting tasks—taking phone messages, to continue with that example—into fun activities. In addition, Wes finds that Gina's gamelike approach to the relationship is a refreshing change of pace from the extremely serious relationships in which he is usually involved. Occasionally, however, Wes believes that Gina regards the relationship as nothing more than a game; even worse, he sometimes thinks that her feelings for him are not so different from her feelings for any one of her many racquetball opponents. On those occasions, he wonders if the only pleasure she gets from the relationship is in beating him at something.

Gina finally comes out to the car, where Wes is still thinking about how appropriate her vanity license plate—IWIN2—is. She flashes a smile of embarrassment as she puts a hand on his knee. She apologizes to him for her behavior and compliments him on his terrific shot. He shakes his head and asks her why she couldn't have said that sooner, rather than destroy his one moment of glory. She responds by telling him that he knows how competitive she can get, and how he has seen it get the best of her before. He nods and smiles, realizing that this is why he is still going out with her. After all, if it really were the case that Gina thought of him as no more than an opponent in a competition, he probably would have stopped seeing her a long time ago.

Modes of Thought and Behavior

In a game story, an individual thinks of a relationship in terms of winning and losing. Gamesters tend to be competitive, and this competitiveness can come out in a sport, as in the case of Gina and Wes's racquetball game, or in the relationship itself, as in the cases both of Jill and Stephen and of Gina and Wes.

Games can take a number of different forms. For one thing, they can be inwardly directed, as with Jill and Stephen and with Gina and Wes. In inwardly directed games, the partners concentrate on each other as game players, and both partners are typically aware that games are being played. In outwardly directed games, third parties (and possibly fourth and fifth parties) can also become involved. In such games—illustrated by *Who's Afraid of Virginia Woolf?*—the game is more complex, more intricate, and potentially more destructive, because typically only some of the players are fully aware that a game is being played.

Games can easily become destructive and be inherently unfair when not everyone knows that a game is being played or, if they do know, what the rules are. The partner who does not know the rules or even that he or she is part of a game is at a major competitive disadvantage and can easily be taken advantage of. If and when the game is discovered, the relationship may be quickly shattered.

Games can also differ in their intensity. They can range from rather minor diversions involving lighthearted humor, to serious and elaborate games where the boundaries between reality and fantasy begin to blur. These games often involve a triangulation of three people in a relationship.

Another dimension along which games differ is whether the competitors are real or fantasy individuals. Couples sometimes invent false players and competitors who may, for example, be competing for the affection of one or both partners. The other partner may therefore find himself or herself competing against someone who does not exist. One partner may invent a person or the suggestion of a person, who is presented as real, in order to pique the other partner's interest or jealousy.

The game mentality can be turned into another and usually more constructive form when the couple perceive themselves as being on the same side of a game that they are playing with others. For example, in doubles tennis, a couple may compete against another couple, trying together to win against the outsiders. In other forms of games, however, the outsiders may not realize they are being drawn into a game or, having realized it, may not wish to play.

Complementary Roles: Winner and Loser

Because games typically involve two people playing against each other, there is likely to be a winner and a loser. In lighthearted games, neither partner takes seriously who wins or loses. In more serious games, however, the stakes can be increased, so that partners are competing as fiercely as they might in tournament tennis. Such competitive relationships tend to be at risk because they can be so stressful, and because one individual may truly feel like a loser (and be perceived in that way by the other individual).

When partners play on the same team (as in the doubles tennis analogy), they may perceive themselves both as potential winners. Their goal, though, is to turn some other individual or individuals into losers, so that the problems that are associated with the game story still arise—they are just displaced outside the relationship.

Advantages and Disadvantages

Gamelike relationships have a sense of excitement, rapid change, and sometimes fun. They may also represent a recognition that life should not be taken all too seriously. At the same time, a game that starts out as being not so serious can become serious and disruptive to the relationship, especially if one or the other partner becomes obsessed with winning. A danger in such relationships is that the game will begin to take over the relationship, and that what comes to be taken seriously is not the intimacy that can be established, but rather the sense of competition. Unless both partners enjoy, or at least can tolerate, such a sense of competition, the relationship is likely to be at risk.

COORDINATION STORIES

In coordination stories, love is viewed as evolving as partners work together to create or maintain something. In a travel story, the partners view their relationship as a journey, with or without a clearly specified destination. In a sewing and knitting story, the partners view themselves as sewing or knitting together their relationship, usually designing the relationship as they piece it together; or one person may do the sewing for the other. In a garden story, the couple views the relationship as being like a garden, which needs to be carefully watered and tended in order to nurture it and make sure it grows. In a business story, the partners see the relationship much as they would see a business, and they act as business partners trying to develop a successful, flourishing business enterprise. In an addiction story, an addict and a codependent feed off each other, basing the relationship around the addict's desperate need for the codependent, and the codependent's need for someone to be addicted to him or her.

THE TRAVEL STORY

In the travel story, an individual views love as a journey that two people take together. There are many different possible destinations, perhaps an unlimited number. The couple has the ability to choose the destination to which they wish to travel.

An important feature of the travel story is the emphasis not just on the destination, but on how to get there, where to stop along the way, and at what speed to take the journey. In many instances, a couple may decide that the destination doesn't much matter, because they are in the relationship to enjoy traveling together rather than to obsess over the particular place in which they hope to end up.

Travel stories tend to succeed as long as they represent a process of becoming. Should the couple actually ever arrive at the destination they set out for, they would likely become bored and need either a fresh destination or a fresh relationship. Because traveling is the theme of the story, arrival poses a problem rather than providing any kind of a goal or final state for the relationship.

Sometimes the travel metaphor takes a more or less literal form, and the couple decides that they enjoy traveling together to new and exciting places. In these cases, the trip is not just a trip per se, but an integral part of the relationship the couple has and of the life they have together.

Diagnosing the Travel Story

1 I believe that, in a good relationship, partners change and grow together.
2 I believe love is a constant process of discovery and becoming.
3 I believe that beginning a relationship is like starting a new journey that promises to be both exciting and challenging.
4 I consider my partner and myself travel companions who go through the journey of life together.
5 In my close relationship, my partner and I look forward to exploration and discovery of what life has to offer.
6 I believe change and discovery are key to the success of my relationship with my partner.
7 I have found my relationship to be a constant process of change and discovery.
8 I enjoy traveling all of life's journeys together with my partner.

Colleen and Rasheed

Colleen and Rasheed work together at a bookstore. Over the past couple of weeks, they have become very friendly on the job, and Colleen is considering whether she should ask Rasheed out. She knows that a relationship with a coworker can cause problems—especially if it does not go well—but she feels that it would be worse to pass up a promising opportunity. So one night, when she sees that he is not busy, she decides to approach him; however, before Colleen can speak, Rasheed asks her if she would like to go out sometime. Needless to say, the two are excited by their mutual interest in each other, and both of them believe that a fulfilling relationship may lie ahead.

As the weeks go by, Colleen and Rasheed become even closer than they had thought they would. In fact, when they are working together at the bookstore, they feel suffocated by the false professionalism they are forced to maintain; they wish that they could display more affection on the job, but they know that their boss would not tolerate such behavior.

The situation becomes so stifling that they consider quitting their jobs and moving on. Colleen tells Rasheed of her desire to drive across the country and work in some small diner in the middle of nowhere. Rasheed shares Colleen's passion for adventure, and together they fantasize about starting up their own little restaurant in a small southwestern town. They recognize that they stand a lot to lose by trying to turn this fantasy into a reality, but it is a risk they are both willing to take. After all, they are no longer getting any fulfillment from their jobs, and they have grown tired of their hometown. More important, they are starting to fall in love with one another, and they do not want to put their relationship in jeopardy by remaining in such a sterile environment. They want their relationship to grow, and they feel a change is necessary to facilitate that growth.

Colleen and Rasheed realize that they cannot just drop everything and leave right away. They first need to save up some more money so that they can at least pay for the trip to the Southwest and have something left over to start the business when they arrive there. The weeks at the bookstore pass more slowly than ever, but Colleen and Rasheed remain happy by focusing on the future and planning for their adventure, leading very frugal lives in order to save up the money they need.

They no longer go out at night, and they have cut down on unnecessary expenditures. They now spend their spare time together doing more unconventional things. They realize that it does not matter what they do, so long as they do it together. Moreover, even if there were no financial concerns, they would still feel it necessary to change their routine, because they do not want their relationship to become stagnant.

After a couple of months of budget-conscious living, Colleen and Rasheed have accumulated enough money to begin their journey. They quit their jobs, pack their belongings into Rasheed's truck, and set out for the Southwest. They understand that the road ahead will hold many obstacles, and that their fantasy of setting up a restaurant together may never materialize. They both believe, however, that if things do not work out with the restaurant, there will be another adventure waiting for them, perhaps somewhere else, and that—as with their daily activities in their hometown—the important thing is not what they do, but that they do it together.

Andy and Stacey

Andy and Stacey are seniors in college. Both realize that there is life after college, and because of the strong feelings they have for each other, they hope to make their relationship last beyond graduation. They recognize that this goal will involve a considerable amount of planning, but they both feel that the continuing success of their relationship is worth the effort.

As they plan for the future, they understand that the most important thing for their relationship is that it continue to grow. They also realize that if it becomes stagnant, they will eventually get bored with one another and choose to move on to something else.

At the moment, Andy and Stacey are trying to decide where they should go to graduate school. Andy was accepted into all of the schools to which he applied, including his top choice. He and Stacey had hoped to go there together, but unfortunately Stacey was rejected. She did, however, get into the graduate program that is Andy's second choice, and it is almost certain that Stacey will go there. Stacey does not want to pressure Andy into settling for his second choice, although she would be happy if they were to wind up at the same school, because it would make it much easier for them to stay together.

Andy wants to be as close to Stacey as possible, but he has been dreaming of going to his top choice since he was a little boy, and he has worked so hard to get in. After much consideration, he decides to go to the program of his dreams, but he assures Stacey that this plan will not interfere with their relationship. After all, it is not as though the two universities are on opposite sides of the country.

Although Andy and Stacey have often heard that relationships between people separated by distance rarely last more than a year, Andy assures Stacey that this will not be the case for them. In fact, he believes that the separation will enhance their relationship rather than detract from it. He argues that if they were to be at the same school, there would not be as much room for change and growth in their relationship, because they would be experiencing the same things. In being apart, they will each have a chance to be surrounded by a different world, and with the knowledge and wisdom that they gain from their respective worlds, they will be able to have many stimulating conversations. Hence, as they develop and grow as individuals, they will develop and grow as a couple as well. Moreover, the effort it will take to keep their relationship strong will remind them of how important they are to each other, so that they will not take the relationship for granted.

Andy and Stacey recognize that they are at a time in their lives when it seems as though there is always a new avenue for them to explore. They understand that if their relationship is to last, their needs for development and growth will eventually have to give way to some sort of constancy. However, they also realize that, even if their relationship comes to a point where they do not have exciting decisions to make, such as where to go to graduate school or what to do with their lives, there will still be room for a different type of growth—an inner, more spiritual growth, which they hope they will be able to experience together.

Modes of Thought and Behavior

The principal characteristic of the travel story is the view of love as a journey that two people take together. The two individuals need not be physically proximate. Thus, Colleen and Rasheed literally go on a journey together, whereas Andy and Stacey are actually planning to be apart physically. In both cases, though, the real journey is something that they construct in their own minds and then implement as part of a life plan.

The travel story is one of the oldest and most common, in that references to it can be found throughout literature almost without regard to how far back one goes in time.[1] It has a great potential for success, so long as the couple can agree on a path, a rate at which to go along the path, and perhaps a destination. Often the decisions about where to go and how to get there change along the way, but again, more important than the decision itself is that both members of the couple support the decision and work to implement it.

Complementary Roles: Two Travelers

Typically, the two roles in a travel story are coordinate—two travelers passing through life together. Within this general framework, there can be many differentiations. For example, one may more often serve as guide or navigator, while the other is pilot or perhaps passenger. The roles complement each other if the two individuals can agree, at some level, on what they will be.

Advantages and Disadvantages

Travel stories that last beyond a very short amount of time generally have a favorable prognosis, because if the travelers can come to an accord on a destination, path, and rate of travel, they are already a long way toward success. If they can't, they often find out quite quickly that they want different things from the relationship, and split up.

Travel relationships tend to be dynamic and focus on the future. They may or may not involve planning, but if they do, then the couple needs a coordinated strategy in order to do the planning. In this sense, they are quite different from a couple playing out a history story, where the focus is more on the past.

The greatest risk in a travel story is that over time one or both partners will change the destination or path they desire. At this point, they may feel as though their paths are diverging. When people speak of growing apart, they often mean that the paths they want to travel along no longer are the same ones. In such cases, the relationship either breaks up or is likely to become increasingly unhappy.

☞ THE SEWING AND KNITTING STORY

In a sewing and knitting story, love is viewed as whatever the couple makes it; it is completely a construction.[1] People create relationships much as they create garments. The design you choose to sew or knit, and how you choose to sew or knit it, is up to you. You can follow a preestablished pattern, or you can design your own pattern, but in either case, it is your decision, along with that of your partner. And each relationship, just like each garment, is unique in both its design and its process of construction. Even if it is similar in some ways to other relationships, it will also inevitably be different from them, because there is no automatic "sewing machine" to render garments identical to each other.

Diagnosing the Sewing and Knitting Story

1   I think your love life is whatever you make it.
2   I think we create for ourselves the kind of relationship that we like to be involve in.
3   I believe the kind of relationship we are in is indicative of the kind of love we seek.
4   I believe involvement in a close relationship is like sewing a dress or a shirt; it i in your own hands to make it fit just right.
5   I believe selecting partners is like knitting a sweater for yourself; it is up to you t find the pattern that will fit you the best.
6   I think it is entirely up to the individual to create his or her own unique relationship.
7   I can make my relationship into whatever I want it to be.
8   I can construct any kind of relationship I want with my partner.

Jesse and Nicole

Jesse and Nicole walk hand in hand out of Mr. Peterman's English class. It is their last class of the day, and because it is Friday, the afternoon and evening are completely free. As they walk to Nicole's car, they try to figure out what they are going to do. Unlike most couples, Jesse and Nicole will probably do something other than see a movie or go to a party. They decided early on that their relationship would not fit into the conventional, preprogrammed notion of what a couple should be. Jesse and Nicole would rather create their own unique relationship.

After going over several options, Jesse and Nicole decide to have an evening picnic at the beach. They bring several candles, some sandwiches, and a blanket to sit on. They settle down in a spot among the dunes, protected from the wind, and watch the dark waves crashing on the shore. After finishing the sandwiches, they lift their plastic cups of soda and make a toast to their relationship. Lying on the blanket, they stare at the stars and philosophize about their place in the world—how in the grand scheme of things they may be meaningless, but to each other they are of such great value. They comment on how wonderful it is that they have been able to stray from the conventional standard of love, with its flowers and fancy dinners. Had they followed that model, they would not be able to do what they are doing now—picnicking on the beach, staring up at the stars.

A few minutes later, Jesse and Nicole have gotten into a rare argument. The high-school prom is in two weeks, and Jesse does not want to go; he considers it to be a complete sham, where a bunch of eighteen-year-olds get dressed up in fancy clothing, get wasted, and dance around a gigantic, pretentious ballroom for hours, then pass out on their beds in the hotel. He believes that he and Nicole should use the night to do something special—something that no couple has ever done before. Nicole is not so crazy about proms, either, but she thinks they should go, mostly to please their parents. She maintains that they can go and still not be like everyone else.

Jesse and Nicole understand that if they had a conventional relationship, they would not be having arguments like this one, in which they cannot decide what new form their love should take. Indeed, if they followed the normal order of things, they would not be having an argument about whether they should go to the prom. After all, every couple goes to the prom, right? What other couples do doesn't matter much to Jesse and Nicole, though.

Jesse and Nicole recognize that their love for each other is more important than the occasional dispute they might have about what to do with their time together. Ordinarily, their arguments do not last long, and they almost never turn into shouting matches. For the most part, Jesse and Nicole are usually able to reach a compromise with which they are both satisfied. In this case, Jesse gives in to Nicole's wish to go to the prom, but he tells Nicole that he refuses to wear a tuxedo, and will not put even one foot on the dance floor, much less two. Nicole starts laughing when she hears Jesse's stipulations, picturing her boyfriend going to the prom in baggy shorts and a ripped T-shirt. Nevertheless, she tells him that he can wear whatever he wants; moreover, she says that she will also wear something completely unconventional. She warns him, though, that she might ask him for a dance, and that he can then decide whether to accept or reject her request.

Susie and Arnold

Susie and Arnold are trying to decide where they should go for their weekend getaway. They certainly do not want to go to some generic, overcrowded vacation spot. For them, the whole idea of a getaway is to leave their monotonous, ordinary existence behind; going to a place where everyone else goes just shifts that existence to a different location. Susie and Arnold do not want their relationship to become a series of stereotyped rituals; they prefer to do things their own way.

At the moment, however, they are having trouble figuring out a place to go that would qualify as a unique getaway. Arnold looks out of his window in the bedroom where he and Susie are sitting, and suddenly an idea comes to him. With a slight smirk, he points his finger through the window and tells Susie that he has found a place for them to go. Susie walks toward the window and looks to where he is pointing. It is a dive motel, and at the sight of it, Susie starts laughing. Nevertheless, she likes the suggestion and agrees that it would be a good choice. After all, it certainly meets their requirement of doing something different.

Arnold and Susie check into the Sunshine Motel, one of many roach motels in their neighborhood. As they walk into their room, Arnold cannot resist performing a belly flop on the bed. Susie laughs hysterically as she watches her twenty-seven-year-old boyfriend do his best imitation of a seven-year-old diving into a swimming pool. They are both pleased with their choice for a weekend getaway, although they understand that most couples would consider it a ridiculous waste of time and the little money it is costing. Susie and

Arnold, however, believe that it is not simply what a couple does that makes the relationship an enjoyable one, but also how the couple goes about doing it.

They could just as easily be having fun if they decided to go somewhere else; the important thing is that they recognize the immense range of activities from which they can choose, and that they do not restrict themselves to a standard procedure to follow. What makes their weekend getaway at the motel so much fun is that both Susie and Arnold recognize how unusual such an outing is. Their relationship is so special because they are always creating a new scene for themselves; in this way, they never feel tied down or stuck in the same old pattern.

As the afternoon turns into evening at the Sunshine Motel, Susie and Arnold try to come up with ideas for an evening activity. They could just stay in their room, order a pizza, and watch a movie; however, since it is such a nice night, they decide to drive to the beach to take a walk along the ocean. They get into Arnold's car, conveniently parked on the street between his apartment and the motel, and drive to the beach.

When they arrive at the beach, they take off their shoes and walk down to the ocean's edge. Hand in hand, they stroll along the packed sand, shivering momentarily every time the evening tide rolls in and gently splashes against their feet and ankles. Arnold suggests that they take off their clothes and dive in for a quick swim. Susie thinks he is crazy, insisting that they will both catch pneumonia in the chilly water. Arnold tells her that they will get used to the temperature after they get in, but Susie persists in her opinion.

Interestingly, one of the few types of problems that Susie and Arnold confront in their relationship is disagreement regarding what new scene they should create for themselves. Fortunately, they are usually able to settle their disagreement by arriving at some sort of compromise. This time, however, Susie refuses to meet Arnold halfway. Arnold accepts her refusal, but decides it is only right of him to pick her up with all of her clothes on and run straight for the water.

Modes of Thought and Behavior

The key mode of thought in the sewing and knitting story is that love is whatever the partners make it. Each couple creates its own unique relationship in its own unique way.

Couples with a sewing and knitting story do not feel bound by convention, but their behavior may be either conventional or unconventional. If it is conventional, it is because they have chosen to follow convention rather than because they have just blindly accepted it. The sewing and knitting couple see many options to be available, and they consider that a primary goal of their relationship is to choose from among all the options that are available or create a new one. Jesse and Nicole have different preferences as a couple than Susie and Arnold, but both couples have knit relationships that are unique.

Complementary Roles: Tailors (Knitters), or Tailor and Client

Sewing and knitting relationships can be characterized either by two tailors (knitters), or by a tailor (knitter) and a client who is content to let the tailor (knitter) do most of the designing. In either case, the couple does not feel bound by the conventions of others.

This kind of relationship probably can succeed only when both partners are willing to create their own unique relationship. If one partner feels bound to convention and the other does not, there is likely to be a great deal of frustration for both persons.

Advantages and Disadvantages

The sewing and knitting story is one of the most creative kinds of stories, at least potentially. It allows for a recognition of all the choices that a couple may make in determining where their relationship goes. There are two potential dangers. The first is if only one partner has the story and the other feels bound by conventions the tailor (knitter) cannot accept. The second potential danger is that both partners are tailors (knitters) but want to create different garments. They may find that they agree that freedom and creativity are important, but that they are nevertheless unable to agree on what form their relationship should take.

☞ THE GARDEN STORY

In a garden story, the relationship is viewed as a garden that needs continually to be nurtured and otherwise cared for. This kind of relationship is, in some ways, the opposite of some versions of the happily-ever-after fairy tale, where the view is that little or nothing needs to be done in order to ensure the happy continuation of the relationship once it has begun. In garden stories, one or both partners strongly believe that the relationship will survive and thrive only if it is carefully watered, provided with abundant sun, and never allowed to become choked with weeds or attacked by garden pests.

Garden stories tend to be highly adaptive, because almost anything—whether an object or a person—will tend to fare better if it is cared for, and care is what gardening stories are about.

Diagnosing the Garden Story

1   I believe a good relationship is attainable only if you are willing to spend the time and energy to care for it, just as you need to care for a garden.
2   I believe any relationship that is left unattended will not survive.
3   I believe relationships need to be nourished constantly in order to survive the ups and downs of life.
4   I believe the secret to a successful relationship is the care that partners take of each other and of their love.
5   I believe no love will survive without constant care and nourishment.
6   I think a love relationship between two people is similar to a delicate flower; it will die if it is left unattended.
7   It is important that I properly nurture and tend to my relationship.
8   I devote a great deal of effort and care to my relationship.

Jim and Elaine

Jim has just come home from a late night at work, and he is totally exhausted. His wife, Elaine, greets him as he walks into the house, and asks him if he is feeling all right. Before he can respond, there is a knock at the door. It is Jim's new secretary, Barbara. Jim left some files at the office, and although Barbara tried to run after him, she could not catch him before he got to the parking lot. She thought that the files might be important, so she decided to come over. Jim is quite grateful for Barbara's diligence and thanks her repeatedly.

Elaine, who has been watching the entire episode unfold, can tell that Barbara is very fond of her husband and in fact might think of him as more than just her boss. Immediately Barbara tries to reflect on the past couple of weeks to see if everything has been going smoothly between her and Jim. Were they talking sufficiently? Were they going out enough? They have always felt that if they do not continually nurture their relationship, problems will almost certainly arise.

Jim and Elaine have been married for fifteen years. Like most couples, they have had their difficulties, but they have always been able to work things out. They believe the reason for their success is the constant attention they pay to their relationship. They understood long ago that the initial intense attraction that existed between them would probably not last forever, and that there would be a considerable amount of work involved in maintaining their love for each other. For instance, whenever they have a problem, they talk about it right away, rather then suppressing it and risking a bigger problem later on. Moreover, they make sure to arrange special occasions throughout the month so that they do not get stuck in the same routine. In the same vein, they often surprise each other with little gifts—reminders of how much they care and think about one another.

After Barbara leaves, Elaine tells Jim her concern about Barbara.

Jim reassures his wife that she is the only woman in his life. He agrees that Barbara is attractive but affirms that he would never let another woman get in the way of the wonderful relationship that they share. Elaine also mentions her concern that perhaps they have not been tending to the relationship as much as they normally do. Jim acknowledges that Elaine might be right, and adds that maybe the care they have provided for their relationship in the past couple of weeks has lacked spontaneity. After all, doing something on the spur of the moment often helps rekindle the initial spark that got them together in the first place. With this in mind, Jim suggests that they go on a little vacation. Elaine is all for the idea, and together they discuss where they should go.

Kelly and Martin

Kelly and Martin are having trouble deciding on how they should rearrange their living room. Ordinarily, neither Kelly nor Martin would care that much about such a trivial issue, and they realize that their indecision probably has something to do with an underlying tension that exists between them. They have both had rough weeks at work, and each of them is feeling quite irritable. Kelly suggests that they put the question of how they should arrange their living room on hold; she feels that it is more important that they sit down and try to figure out what it is that might be troubling them. Kelly and Martin believe that whenever a problem arises in their relationship, they should talk about it and do their best to solve it together. They liken their relationship to a beautiful rosebush, which needs to be nurtured and tended if it is to survive.

Kelly and Martin have not always felt this way about their relationship. In the first few years of their marriage, whenever a problem would arise, they would just sit back and hope that it would go away. However, after the birth of their second child, they started to have some trouble with their marriage. They were spending very little time together, and there was much tension between them. To make matters worse, the time they *were* spending together was never really exciting or enjoyable. They both realized that if they were to return to the happier days that they had once had, they would need to spend more time on their relationship. Because neither of them wanted their marriage to become destructive, especially for the sake of their children, they decided that they should always discuss any problems or issues that concerned them. Moreover, because they knew that nurturing their relationship would take more than just correcting problems once they arose, Kelly and Martin tried to plan entertaining evenings around their demanding work and child care schedules, so as to make their marriage more enjoyable. They understood that, as with taking care of a rosebush, preventing a problem from arising is just as important as curing a problem that already exists.

Kelly and Martin's decision to nurture their relationship on a regular basis has turned out to be a wonderful one. They both believe that it has not only saved their marriage, but also led to a wonderful relationship. Even after they got beyond the initial difficulties that plagued them following the birth of their second child, they still felt that they should continue to approach their marriage in the same way. After all, Kelly and Martin knew that other problems would always arise, and that even when things were going well, it would always be difficult to maintain a strong relationship unless they continually worked at it.

As they now sit and discuss the issues that are troubling them, Martin and Kelly pause for a moment to smile at each other. It is a smile of recognition—a recognition of the importance of their love for each other. There have, of course, been problems along the way, and they both know that there are many still to come; but they also know that as long as they continue to make their relationship a priority, they will be able to get through pretty much anything.

Modes of Thought and Behavior

In a garden story, the partners recognize that a relationship needs continually to be nurtured and attended to, much as one would care for the flowers in a garden. The partners therefore take relatively little for granted and do what they can to ensure that the relationship, like a flower garden, will flourish and survive the various kinds of adversity that are inevitable in life.

Garden stories tend to be adaptive, because relationships usually do need the care and attention that gardeners are willing to put into them. These relationships are particularly likely to become what is sometimes called *companionate,* where the partners view each other as best friends.[1] John Lee used the Greek term *storge* to refer to a friendship kind of love.[2] What such relationships may lack in passion, however, they may more than make up for in durability.

Complementary Roles: Gardeners, or Gardener and Flower

Typically, people view themselves as dual gardeners maintaining a flower garden. At times, however, one of the individuals may view him- or herself as the gardener, and the other individual as the garden or as a flower in the garden. In the latter case, most of the caring is directed from one individual to the other. The gardener-garden relationship is not like the collector-collectible relationship, however, because the gardener does not have the sense of possession that the collector has, and the flower is alive, whereas there is a more objectlike quality to the elements in a collection.

Advantages and Disadvantages

The biggest advantage of a garden story is its recognition of the importance of caring and nurturance. No other kind of story involves quite the constant caring and attention that is found in a garden relationship.

The biggest potential disadvantage is the danger that, over time, a lack of spontaneity or even boredom will develop. People in garden stories are not immune to the lure of extramarital relationships, for example, and at times get involved in them to generate excitement, even though they may still highly value their primary relationship.

In getting involved in other relationships, however, they are usually putting the primary relationship at risk.

A second potential disadvantage is that of smothering—that the attention just becomes too much, or too all-consuming. Just as one can overwater a flower, so one can overwater a relationship. One therefore needs to know when just to let things be and allow rain and nature to take their course.

☞ THE BUSINESS STORY

In the business story, a relationship is run much like a business. An individual is attracted to a mate as a potential "business partner," who is evaluated largely in terms of his or her suitability in this role. Thus, a careful weighing of economic considerations, social status, and business sense may play more of a role in the formation of this kind of relationship than they would in the formation of other kinds of relationships.

Diagnosing the Business Story

1 I believe close relationships are partnerships, just like most business relationship

2 I believe close relationships are not only about love, but also about running a household financially.

3 I believe one of the most important issues in a close relationship is the making a spending of money.

4 I believe that in a romantic relationship, just as in a job, both partners should perform their duties and responsibilities according to their "job description."

5 Whenever I consider having a relationship with someone, I always consider the financial implications of the relationship as well.

6 When all is said and done, I believe economic considerations are of key importance to a relationship.

7 I believe relationships are in many ways like a well-run business.

8 I believe a good relationship is at its core a business proposition.

David and Meredith

David and Meredith have been married for six years. Just about everyone who knows them regards the marriage as a perfect success. Indeed, they are always on top of their bills, they almost never argue, and their daughter, Mary, is a little angel. Today is Sunday, which means they are busy balancing their budget and planning for the week ahead. David's job is to handle all of the financial matters. First he pays the bills and tallies up the expenditures from the previous week; then, taking these outlays into consideration, he calculates a precise amount of money to be put aside for Mary's college fund; finally, he tentatively plans how much money will be spent in the upcoming week. Meredith is in charge of the other family affairs. First, she decides who will be responsible for taking care of Mary's various needs; next, she makes a list of household chores, assigning a specific person to each task and indicating the date and time that the tasks are to be performed. Occasionally, of course, a problem arises during the week that interferes with their plans. When such a situation occurs, both David and Meredith sit down and discuss ways to confront and deal with the problem.

Perhaps the only person who does not think their marriage is a perfect success is David's younger brother, Jimmy. Jimmy is a bit on the romantic side, and he often asks his brother how he could possibly tolerate such a dull, impersonal relationship. David tells him that he regards the relationship as efficient rather than dull, although he admits that there is little romance between him and his wife. Jimmy considers this depiction to be a gross understatement; according to him, his brother's marriage is more like a series of agreements between two business partners than it is a bond between husband and wife. Interestingly enough, David does not deny this assertion. He maintains, however, that their businesslike relationship provides several important benefits: It maintains the financial stability of the family, and it ensures that Mary's overall welfare is always closely guarded.

David has explained to Jimmy that, in the early stages of their marriage, both he and Meredith felt that their frivolous needs for excitement and adventure should be put on hold until the more essential needs, such as financial security and family planning, were taken care of. This sort of attitude permeated their entire relationship, including their sex life, and by the time things were going smoothly, they really did think of themselves as business partners as well as husband and wife. They would have regarded it as unnatural suddenly to change the pattern of their marriage; they had simply become too accustomed to their efficient, methodical way of living. David believes that the love in his marriage lies in his and Meredith's shared interest in the family's well-being, rather than in a passionate interest in one another.

Warren and Kathy

Warren sits on his side of the bed, evening out his fingernails with a nail file. He is wearing his blue pajamas—the same style that he has worn most nights for the past fifteen years. His wife, Kathy, sits on the other side of the bed; in one hand she holds a small mirror, while with the other she gently rubs a moisturizing cream into her cheeks and forehead. She is wearing a pink nightgown that, like her husband's blue pajamas, is the same style she's worn for years. After they finish their respective evening rituals, Warren and Kathy wish each other a pleasant if dispassionate goodnight. Warren switches off the light on his side of the bed, and Kathy does the same on hers. Without any visible sign of affection, they fall asleep on their separate sides, facing in opposite directions.

Warren and Kathy have been married for twenty-one years. Warren is a major executive in a marketing firm, and Kathy is a prestigious defense attorney. Needless to say, they are very well-off; nevertheless, they both agree that there is no such thing as being too secure financially. Indeed, with the increasing costs of living and college tuition (they have two children who will soon be entering private colleges), not to mention Warren and Kathy's desire to retire at a relatively early age, money is in high demand. Therefore, even with the high family income, they are extremely money-conscious, organizing their lives around their various economic needs and wishes. They spend a lot of time managing and investing their income, planning their expenditures, and keeping a close watch over all of their financial transactions throughout the month. Warren and Kathy divide these various responsibilities equally between themselves, in order to ensure that overall efficiency is maximized.

Their relationship is in many ways like a business proposition. They are both dedicated to ensuring the economic security of the family, which they value more than anything else. This businesslike relationship, which is highly successful when it comes to financial matters, is not what anyone, including themselves, would call romantic. As evidenced by their bedtime ritual, Warren and Kathy value things other than romance. The issue of romance may have been raised once, or at most twice, in their twenty-one years of marriage. They simply value the family's economic well-being more than they value a passionate, romantic marriage. For them, what they have works.

Modes of Thought and Behavior

People with a business story see an intimate relationship the way they would a business partnership. Warren and Kathy, and David and Meredith, pretty much see their relationships in this way. Indeed, to them, a relationship *is* a business, and the story of love is a story about successfully running a business. The relationship tends to involve what John Lee has called a *storge* style of interrelating: The partners have a friendship type of love.[1] Such relationships tend to be warm rather than hot, and companionate rather than passionate.[2]

All of us, of course, evaluate a potential intimate partner for suitability. But people looking for a business story from the start tend more to emphasize the criteria that one would look for in a business partner, including financial ones. What some might view as dull or boring, they view as responsible, as in the case of Warren and Kathy.

A relationship that starts off in another way can shade into a business story, often without the partners being fully aware of what is happening. As the demands of everyday life creep into the relationship—financial demands, demands of organizing a household, and perhaps demands of balancing home and work—businesslike aspects of the relationship can become more and more salient; eventually they may take over. Some couples fight this tendency, perhaps seeking ways to maintain or, if necessary, rekindle romance. Others may feel comfortable with what is happening, viewing it as the natural course close relationships take.

Complementary Roles: Business Partners, or Employer and Employee

The most common roles in a business story are those of business partners, with the partners trying to maximize whatever it is they value—money for many, but fame or a glitzy lifestyle for others. In a partnership, each individual contributes roughly equally to the business arrangement.

Another possible arrangement is one in which, effectively, one individual becomes the boss and the other individual the employee. In such cases, the boss dominates the relationship, and the partners construct a relationship in which one individual holds more power in the business and perhaps partakes more in the rewards that the business reaps. The danger of such an arrangement is self-evident: feelings of exploitation, which may well be justified.

Other potential, more differentiated roles may develop as well. For example, one individual may take on more of the role of chief executive officer, or chief financial officer, or chief operations officer, or whatever. David, for example, takes on the role of chief financial officer; Meredith, that of chief operations officer. A major issue in the success of these relationships is mutual satisfaction with the roles in terms of the sharing of power and responsibility.

Advantages and Disadvantages

A business story has several potential advantages, not the least of which is that the bills are more likely to get paid than in many other kinds of relationships. The reason is that someone is always minding the store, making sure both that they get paid and that the money is there to pay them in the first place. Another potential advantage is that the roles tend to be more clearly defined than in many other kinds of relationships. The partners are also in a good position to "get ahead" in terms of whatever it is that they want, and they are in a good position to unite against threats from other "businesses," which they are likely to see as competitive, whether or not they are. Other "businesses" might include other couples attempting to achieve greater worldly success or individual rivals trying to steal away one or the other of the partners from the business.

One potential disadvantage is particularly highlighted if only one of the two partners sees their love relationship as a business story. The other partner may quickly become bored with the relationship and look for interest and excitement outside the marriage. The story can also turn sour if the distribution of authority or the roles in general do not satisfy one or both partners. If the partners cannot work out mutually compatible roles, they may find themselves spending a lot of time fighting for the kind of position they want in the business. It is important in such relationships to maintain the option of flexibility, so that if one or the other partner tires of the way the roles are distributed, other kinds of roles for each of the partners at least can be considered. Problems arise, of course, when one individual is happy with the roles and the other is eager to change them.

☞ THE ADDICTION STORY

In an addiction story, an individual feels addicted to his or her partner, much in the same way the individual might feel addicted to a drug. Loss of the partner results in withdrawal symptoms, just as a person would experience withdrawal from a drug. It is not the common fear of being alone that drives the addiction, but rather, the need for the particular partner. That partner, in turn, may relish the role of being needed in such an extreme and uncompromising way.

Diagnosing the Addiction Story

1   I cannot imagine my love life without my partner.
2   I would be a desperate person without my partner.
3   For me, the necessity of having my partner around is like the necessity of havin
    air to breathe.
4   I don't think I could live without my partner.
5   My life would be meaningless without my partner's love.
6   If my partner were to leave me, my life would be completely empty.
7   I could not survive without my partner.
8   I am almost totally dependent on my partner for my happiness.

Amanda and Kevin

It looks as though Amanda will finally be able to get some sleep. For the past several hours, she has been on the phone with her boyfriend, Kevin, who is spending a couple of weeks with his grandmother in Louisiana. Amanda and Kevin are both college juniors and have been going out since they were sixteen. When the two are at school, or anywhere else for that matter, they are practically inseparable—in fact, this is the first time in almost three years that they have been apart for more than a week. Naturally, this separation has been hard on both of them; however, it has been harder on Kevin. Kevin has always felt a need to be with Amanda, and whenever they are not together, he becomes preoccupied with the thought of losing her. Over the past ten days, he has been calling her constantly; they talk about many things, but Kevin always ends the conversation by asking Amanda to reassure him that she will never leave him.

Although Amanda is also having trouble being without Kevin, there have been several times this past week that she has felt quite uneasy with some of the things that he has said to her over the phone. For instance, it makes her feel very uncomfortable when he tells her that he could not survive without her. When the two are together, Amanda obviously recognizes Kevin's strong attachment to her, but his dependency is not as conspicuous because she is there for him. As a result, she sees his attachment as a sign of his strong love for her, rather than as a neurotic need for her always to be around.

Over the phone, however, she cannot be oblivious to his dependency, and she is not exactly sure how she should handle it. At the moment she certainly wants to be with Kevin, and she hopes that their relationship will last forever; however, she recognizes that human emotions are hardly static, and that there may come a time when she no longer wants to be with him. Just thinking about this possibility makes her feel very guilty, and she wonders what would happen to him if she eventually decided to end the relationship.

Amanda wakes up at noon the next day and is surprised to discover that Kevin has not yet called her. She wonders if everything is all right and tries to contact him. Nobody is home, and so she figures that he must have gone out for a little while. She walks over to her desk and looks at a picture of Kevin that she has on display; as she does so, she begins to miss him terribly, and realizes that he might not be alone in his dependency. She always thought that the reason she spent so much time with him was simply because she loved him—which was the same reason, she felt, why he was attached to her. However, she now recognizes that she might be as dependent on him as he is on her, and she believes that the awkward reaction she had to some of his comments on the phone might simply reflect her fear that these comments apply as much to her as they do to him.

Before Amanda can continue her self-analysis, the phone rings. She eagerly picks it up and is quite relieved when she hears Kevin's voice on the other end. It turns out that he and his grandmother had decided to go on a morning boat ride. Amanda and Kevin talk for several hours, but this time Amanda does not feel uncomfortable when Kevin explains how much he needs her. In fact, she tells him the same thing.

Melanie and Jason

Standing on the train platform, Melanie urges her husband, Jason, to reconsider his decision to visit an old friend in New York. Jason explains that he must go, because this is the last opportunity that he will have in quite some time to see his friend. He emphasizes, however, that he will be gone for only six days and that he will call her every night. Sensing that he is not about to change his mind, Melanie breaks into a frightful sweat; she tells Jason all the horrible things that might happen to him while he is in New York, and she asks him to think about what would happen to her if something were to go wrong. He assures her that everything will be fine and kisses her good-bye. With tears running down her cheeks, she watches him board the train, following him with her eyes as he walks down the aisle. She waits there until the train is just a tiny speck in the distance.

Melanie drives home, wondering how she is going to make it through the next few days. She can be comfortable only when Jason is around; without him, she feels unsure of herself, and finds it difficult to handle even the simplest of tasks. To make matters worse, she has already imagined several situations that would result in Jason's never returning—everything from his getting shot and killed on the subway to his falling in love with someone else and leaving her forever. In all of these cases, she would be forced to live without him, a situation that she cannot see herself being able to manage. She is completely dependent on him—not only for security and companionship, but for taking care of most of the family's needs as well.

When Jason arrives in New York, he is excited to see his old friend, and the two of them go out to dinner. For the most part, he is happy to get away from Melanie for a few days. He loves her, but occasionally her dependency on him makes him feel suffocated: He has to spend an inordinate amount of time with her, and he must always be on guard to avoid saying anything that might make her suspect that he no longer wants to be with her. Even something as seemingly innocuous as wanting to watch a baseball game with a friend is often interpreted as a sign that he no longer loves her. In short, being in New York gives Jason a sense of freedom that he rarely feels when he is at home.

There is a part of Jason, however, that does not want to be away from Melanie. Even though her clinging behavior is often terribly confining, there are some aspects of it that, over the years, he has come to depend upon. For instance, her anxious attachment makes him feel loved and wanted; when he does not have her around, he loses the sense of importance that these feelings give him. Even as he eats dinner with his friend, he wishes his wife were beside him to tell him how much she loves him, or to ask him what she should order. He is no longer enjoying himself as much as he did at the beginning of the meal, and he has already begun to think about calling her. Jason would prefer it if he and his wife were not so dependent on each other, but he also recognizes that it would be worse if they felt no attachment at all.

Modes of Thought and Behavior

The key feature of the addiction story is strong, anxious attachment to a partner, or the need to have such an attachment. Once the person becomes attached, he or she seems to cling for dear life. The thought of losing the partner can literally send the person into a panic. The addict is likely to feel that he or she just couldn't survive without the partner; if they lose the person, they experience withdrawal symptoms, and it is for this reason that psychologists caution clients against addictive relationships.[1] Melanie is experiencing withdrawal, even though her husband has just left, and will soon be returning.

My own "triangular theory of love"—according to which different kinds of love involve different combinations of intimacy, passion, and commitment—views passion as driven by psychophysiological arousal, which tends to show a consistent course that is much like that of addictions.[2] According to the theory, passion can be aroused very rapidly upon meeting or even seeing a person. There is a strong positive force that leads one to feel passionate toward a person—love at first sight, as it is often called. As time goes on, however, an opposing force starts to come into being, moderating the experience of passion. The process is much like that with any addiction (to coffee, alcohol, or whatever), whereby as time passes, the amount of stimulation initially needed to produce a high no longer produces the same feeling. The result is that one reaches a kind of equilibrium, where the addiction remains but the experience of passion is modified. Richard Solomon has proposed a generalized theory of motivation, according to which all addictions can be understood in pretty much the same terms as described here. Indeed, the mechanism described here for a personal addiction is derived from Solomon's theory.[3]

What begins to happen is that the major force driving the addiction is the desire not to experience withdrawal symptoms. People who drink a lot of coffee, for example, may have started drinking coffee to perk themselves up, and later find themselves drinking the coffee routinely just to stay awake. Similarly, the individual addicted to a partner may not feel the addiction in his or her day-to-day life, but may start to panic when the person goes away, or even at the thought of losing the person. What started out as a positive feeling is now an attempt to stave off a negative one—withdrawal symptoms—which is one reason why the prognosis for addictive relationships is not always particularly good.

Complementary Roles: Addict and Codependent

The addiction story, like all stories, has two complementary roles. The first and dominant role is that of the addict—the one who seeks out the relationship and then has great difficulty letting go, even if the relationship is going really badly. The addict is as addicted to the relationship as someone else may be to a drug. Indeed, the addict may have other addictions, because people with addictive personalities often find themselves falling into multiple addictions.

The second role is that of the codependent. This is the person who supports the role of the addict. The codependent feels as though he or she is helping the addict, although the kind of help being offered is not always helpful. The problem is that the codependent often needs the addict as much as the addict needs the codependent. This need is apparent in the cases of both Amanda and Jason. Both see themselves in the roles of codependent, but realize that their need for the addict is about as great as the need of the addict for them. Indeed, they come to realize that, in a sense, they are addicted, too.

The addict gives the codependent a certain kind of meaning in life—a sense of making an important difference to someone. After all, the codependent realizes the addict feels as though he could not live without the codependent. This realization is what Jason experiences on his trip to New York. Without Melanie around, some of the meaning seems to be gone from his life.

The problem is that the needs of the codependent—as in the cases of Amanda and Jason—may feed and support the addiction. The codependent unconsciously helps maintain the behavior that he or she may consciously believe is maladaptive for both of them. The support can take various forms: The codependent may nurture the addiction, or act flattered by it, or pretend to be dissatisfied while covertly showing satisfaction.

So long as both partners are happy with the relationship, there may be no harm done. But if the relationship starts to degenerate, as addictive relationships have a tendency to do, the complementary roles may maintain a relationship that would be better ended. In general, this kind of relationship is not one that has the highest probability of long-term success, simply because addictions of all kinds can have a way of spiraling into destructive behavior patterns.

For example, the addict may constantly need more and more of the codependent, leading the codependent to feel stifled. Seeking some freedom, the codependent may try to create some space and distance. But the effort increases the addict's already high level of anxiety, as the addict begins to worry that he is losing the codependent. The addict then acts in ways that further stifle the codependent, and the spiral of degeneration is soon in full motion. If Kevin becomes more and more possessive of Amanda's time, he might find that Amanda just can't take it anymore, and that she might start to lose interest.

Advantages and Disadvantages

The addiction story has some potential advantages for both partners. The addict may feel a kind of high from a close relationship that relatively few people are able to experience. To the addict, the relationship is literally like a drug, and may even have some of the same physiological effects as certain drugs. To the codependent, the relationship provides a sense of meaning and usefulness. Someone who has felt rather useless may find the role of the codependent especially seductive, for here at long last is a chance to mean something to someone.

NARRATIVE STORIES

In narrative stories, the partners believe there is some kind of real or imagined text, which exists outside the relationship but which is prescriptive in many ways of how the relationship should proceed. In a fantasy story, the text is a fairy tale in which a prince or knight in shining armor rescues or otherwise enters the life of a princess, after which the couple lives happily ever after. In a history story, the text is a history text in which the past provides the guidelines for and the directions to the future. In a science story, scientific laws and principles drive the relationship and what people feel, think, and do in the relationship. In a cookbook story, there exists a recipe that contains all the ingredients for a happy and successful relationship; one need merely follow the recipe to achieve a lifetime of bliss.

THE FANTASY STORY

The fantasy story is perhaps the most classical love story—it is the story of the prince (or knight in shining armor) and the princess in search of each other. Once they find each other, they are, of course, supposed to live happily ever after. People who hold this story are likely to view their partner as their dream come true.

Of course, fantasy stories, like any other stories, can go bad. Princes or knights can turn out secretly to be sorcerers or knaves, just as princesses can be witches in disguise. Those with a fantasy story need to penetrate such disguises before it is too late, in order to ensure that their search has truly yielded what they were seeking.

Diagnosing the Fantasy Story

1 I think fairy tales about relationships can come true.
2 I think people owe it to themselves to wait for the partner they have always dreamed about.
3 I think near-perfect relationships are possible, provided you find that one person who is just right for you.
4 I still believe in the concept of living happily ever after, provided you get to meet your Mr./Ms. Right.
5 I do believe that there is someone out there for me who is my perfect match.
6 I think fairly tales come true for some people every day; there is no reason why mine can't come true for me.
7 I like my relationships to be ones in which I view my partner as something like a prince or princess in tales of old.
8 I think the best relationships truly are like fairy tales.

Greg and Heather

Greg cannot wait to tell his best friend, Mickey, about what has just happened to him. He calls Mickey up and, without asking if he is busy or not, says that he will be coming over in five minutes. At first Mickey is a bit taken aback by Greg's anxious excitement, but he has heard him talk this way before, so he has a pretty good guess as to what his friend is going to tell him. When Greg arrives, Mickey's intuition is immediately confirmed, as his friend begins informing him about the new girl of his dreams.

Greg was walking his dog in the park when all of a sudden this gorgeous woman came up to him and started petting his dog. Her name was Heather, and he knew right away that she was the woman for him. They had a very interesting conversation, and before she left, she gave him her number. The next day he called her, and the two arranged to meet for dinner. Greg is just now on his way to pick her up and he can hardly contain himself. He believes that Heather is the woman he is going to marry, and he has already pictured their wedding.

After hearing Greg tell his story, Mickey shakes his head with a grin, asking Greg if he knows how many times he has told him the same story. Greg insists that this time it is different. He knows that he has had feelings like this about a woman before and that in the past the relationships have never turned out to be as good as he had imagined they would be. However, he has learned from his experiences, and he now knows how to handle the situation better. He is tired of his brief flings and countless failures; he will try harder this time to make everything work out, and he is certain that Heather will be worth all of the trouble.

Mickey still shakes his head and tells Greg that the only way a successful, long-term relationship will ever materialize for him is if he stops living in his fantasies; he begs Greg to understand that nobody will ever stack up to the storybook image of a princess that he creates when he meets someone. Greg isn't listening. This time, he believes, he has found the princess he has been seeking.

Greg continues to describe how terrific Heather is. He tells Mickey of Heather's work at the community center and of her strong affection for children. Greg is convinced that Heather will make the perfect mother. Mickey begins to respond, but before he can get the words out, Greg suddenly realizes what time it is, and tells Mickey that he must leave or else he will be late for his date. First, however, he has to run over to the local flower shop and pick out the finest roses he can find; after all, the girl of his dreams deserves only the best.

Alexis and Cory

It is Saturday night, but Alexis is staying home for the evening. She had planned on going out, but she has had a miserable day. Her boss was dissatisfied with her marketing reports, and she received not one but two speeding tickets. Not being in a festive mood, Alexis decides to watch a movie. She walks up to her video collection and picks out *Cinderella.*

It is Alexis's favorite movie, and although she has seen it dozens of times, she has yet to get tired of it. Whenever she is feeling down, she likes to watch it and pretend that she is Cinderella, who, despite her low status and apparent insignificance in the world, winds up living happily ever after with Prince Charming.

Ever since she was a little girl, Alexis has dreamed of having a fairy-tale romance like Cinderella's. Each time Alexis begins a relationship, she imagines that the man with whom she is involved is a mythical, idyllic prince. Some of Alexis's friends have told her that it is unrealistic to think that such an ideal person exists; as evidence, they point out the fact that none of her past boyfriends or relationships has lived up to her fairy-tale standards. When Alexis thinks about it rationally, she agrees with them. Nevertheless, something in Alexis is convinced that her own Prince Charming is still out there and that one day he will come to her and sweep her off her feet.

While watching *Cinderella,* Alexis starts daydreaming about Cory, a new employee at the office where Alexis works. Alexis has talked with Cory only once, but he made an excellent first impression on her. As Alexis watches the movie unfold, her strong feelings about Cory become even stronger. She starts to wonder if maybe he will become her knight in shining armor. She begins to envision what their relationship would be like. Cory, of course, would be the perfect boyfriend. He would be romantic, caring, and protective. He would always be there for her when she was feeling down, and he would be able to make all of her problems disappear. He would stand by her at all times, and he would defend her whenever she needed him to. They would never fight or argue, and their love for each other would never fade.

As Alexis continues to daydream, the ideal image that she is creating of Cory seems to become more and more realistic to her. She has almost convinced herself that he must be the Prince Charming for whom she has been searching ever since she was a little girl. She imagines him walking into her office on Monday and confessing his love for her. He tells her that she is too special to be working in such a place. Together, they quit their jobs and embark on a new life together. They move to an idyllic cottage in the countryside, where they raise a wonderful family. And, of course, they live happily ever after. It's a fantasy, but Alexis believes it just might come true.

Modes of Thought and Behavior

Many of our fantasy stories about love have their origins in mythology. In the tale of Eros and Psyche, for example, the god Eros chooses a mortal, Psyche, as his lover, but he does not want Psyche to know who he is. He therefore brings her to a wonderful palace to live in bliss, but he insists that it always be dark when they are together and that Psyche not try to see what he looks like or even attempt to figure out who he is.

Psyche is blissfully happy with Eros, but her sisters convince her that something must be amiss and that she really must take a peek. Why else would he not want Psyche to see him? What if he is ugly or deformed or simply evil? Psyche takes a peek by candlelight while Eros sleeps, and discovers his wonderful visage; but she also accidentally drips hot candle wax on him, awakening her lover. Feeling betrayed, Eros flees. Psyche then must meet the greatest challenge of her life—to find him despite the many obstacles placed in her way. Eventually Eros forgives Psyche, they are reunited, and Psyche is transformed into a goddess, to live eternally with Eros on Mt. Olympus.[1]

The theme of the story of Psyche and Eros is a search, and a search is often the theme of fantasy stories. Fantasy stories tend to be about what Francesco Alberoni, an Italian sociologist, calls the *nascent state* of relationships—when a relationship is just beginning and a couple is deeply in love (or one person is in love with the other, whatever the other may feel).[2] It is more difficult to maintain the role of prince or princess once one's partner gets to know one better, but it is not impossible. Sometimes this kind of image is maintained not because of what the partner is like, but in spite of it.

Complementary Roles: Prince and Princess

Individuals with a fantasy story are in search of a prince (knight) or a princess. Sometimes they find the partner of their dreams; more often they do not, or they find a person they initially think is the person of their dreams, only to discover that this is not so. Even if they find the person they have been dreaming of and are relatively happy, they may start fantasizing again, because fairy tales aren't really about living happily ever after (remember that the happily-ever-after part of any classical fairy tale has only one line devoted to it) but are about the search for the partner, often in the face of overwhelming odds.

Either the prince or princess, or both, may be more in love with the idea of the fantasy than with any particular instantiation of it. The result may be a series of repeated disillusionments, as in cases like this almost no relationship can meet the standards to which it is being subjected.

Fantasy roles may convert the prince and princess, at the time of union, into king and queen, after the partners have spent some time together. The problem is that the roles of king and queen almost never have quite the excitement that the roles of prince and princess have. As a result, when the roles start to convert, one or both partners may start to feel dissatisfied. Ironically, the dissatisfaction may not be with the partner per se, but rather with the new roles that a long-term relationship bestows upon both individuals.

Advantages and Disadvantages

The fantasy story can be a particularly powerful one. The individual may feel swept up in the emotion of the search for the perfect partner or of developing the perfect relationship with a partner who has been found. The fantasy may continue forever, but probably only so long as the relationship feels as if it is in a process of becoming, rather than a completed product. It is probably no coincidence that in literature most fantasy stories take place before or outside of marriage: Fantasies are hard to maintain when one has to pay the bills, pack the children off to school, and cope with the bad moods that affect all of us from time to time. To maintain the very happy feeling of the fantasy, therefore, one has to ignore, at least to some extent, the mundane aspects of life.

Fantasy partners often feel a great deal of admiration and respect for each other and are willing to do a great deal to keep their partners happy. They may feel a depth to their love that participants in few other stories may feel. The love, however, may not be as deep as it seems, because the feeling of depth, like the relationship itself, can turn out to be a fantasy as well.

The potential disadvantages of the fantasy relationship are quite plain. The greatest is the possibility for disillusionment when one or the other partner discovers that no one could fulfill the fantastic expectations that have been created. This lack of realism can lead partners to feel dissatisfied with relationships that most others would view as quite successful.

In our own research, we have distinguished between two kinds of ideals: idealistic ideals, of the kind one reads about in fantasy stories or sees in Hollywood movies, and realistic ideals, which are more grounded expectations for what is possible in a relationship.[3] To the extent that a couple can create a fantasy story based on realistic rather than idealistic ideals, they have the potential for success; to the extent that they want to be characters in a myth, chances are that's exactly what they'll get: a myth.

☞ THE HISTORY STORY

In the history story, the present is defined in large part by the past. Couples with a history story view the present as a cumulation of past events and see the past as living on in the present.

People with a history story are record keepers. These records can take either physical or mental forms. For example, these people might be particularly prone to keeping numerous photo albums, video recordings of important events, and perhaps genealogical charts. Or the interest in history may extend only to their own relationship. In such cases, individuals may be as interested in the "bloodlines," or genealogical record, of potential partners as they are in the partners themselves. For example, they may take particular pride that they are or their partner is a descendant of a certain individual, or they may feel a particular shame that they have or their partner has a certain ancestor.

Societies that are highly defined by caste tend to encourage and promote the history story and to view a given relationship as merely one node in a complex network of interrelationships. Certain partners may be forbidden or strongly discouraged because their historical pedigrees do not fit those desired or even required by the family. Royalty, for example, have tended to marry only within approved family lines. The cost of this inbreeding, historically, has often been mental retardation and other genetic defects. These kinds of genetic defects tend to occur when a dangerous recessive gene is paired with the same dangerous recessive in a partner.[1]

Most couples, of course, do not have those worries. Those couples with a history story see their union and their progeny as continuing (or less often, starting) a "stock" or line of descendants whose history is an important part of who they are. Organizations such as the Daughters of the American Revolution (DAR) represent the notion of a continuous and distinguished family line with deep and distinguished historical roots. Some parents with a history story may find that a major determinant of their happiness with their children's marital choice is not the person, per se, but the historical pedigree the person represents; of course, not all couples with a history story care about such lineage. The history they may care about may be their own individual history, rather than that of ancestors before them.

Diagnosing the History Story

1   I often think about all the moments that I have shared with my partner and how much this common history means to me.
2   I believe that to know the future of a relationship, one should look at its past.
3   It is very important to me to keep objects or pictures that remind me of special moments that I have shared with my partner.
4   I believe our past is a very important part of us and our relationships, and that it should never be forgotten.
5   I think anniversaries are especially important because they remind us of our shared history.
6   I like reminiscing about some important past events in our relationship, because I believe our past is an important part of us.
7   I cannot imagine separating our history from our present or future, as our past has become a part of us.
8   I believe a couple's shared past is necessarily of great importance to their present relationship.

Allison and Eric

Allison is extremely upset because her boyfriend, Eric, has recently agreed to work on a four-month movie project in Milan. The two have been arguing all week long, and in an attempt to put an end to the arguments, they decide to go to Inspiration Point in Will Rogers State Park, where Eric first asked Allison out two years ago. Not only would the place serve as a reminder of a happier moment in their lives, but the peaceful surroundings and beautiful view overlooking the city would provide an ideal atmosphere in which to recall many of the events that have shaped their relationship.

Eric and Allison have always felt that reflecting on their past allows them to enhance their perspective on current situations; moreover, if the current situation is a difficult one, seeing it in the broader context of their entire relationship helps them get through the tough times.

Sitting atop Inspiration Point, Allison and Eric reminisce about all they have been through together. Eric stands up and moves closer to the edge of the cliff. Beckoning Allison toward him, he points to a tiny speck in the distance where he believes they went to eat dinner on their first date. Allison argues with him, saying the restaurant is farther to the left than where he is pointing. They laugh over their ridiculous argument, realizing that it would be impossible to identify the actual spot from so far away. Allison turns to him and asks if he remembers how that night ended. Eric shakes his head with a grin, knowing full well that she is referring to the door he closed on her arm as they were leaving the restaurant.

The topic suddenly switches to their current situation. Allison pleads with Eric not to go to Milan. She understands that it is a great opportunity for him, but she points out that everything is going well for him here. Eric tells her that it is more than just a great opportunity; if he does an excellent job in Milan, he is convinced that he will receive a promotion when he returns home. Allison walks away for a minute, and Eric knows that she is thinking about the first time he left to do a project on the road.

Eric was gone for only three weeks, but he had a brief fling with someone while he was away, and Allison is worried that the same thing is going to happen again. Eric walks toward her and suggests that they sit down. He explains to her that what took place the first time he went away will never happen again. After all, at the time, they had only been seeing each other for a relatively short while, and he was not even sure how committed he was to her. Now he is convinced that he loves her, and he believes very strongly that one day they will get married; he says he would never do what he did in the past, because he would not want to jeopardize the wonderful relationship they have. Allison appreciates what he says, but emphasizes the long time that he will be gone, and all the wonderful people that he will meet. She recognizes that the relationship is on a different level than it was the last time he went away, but she also knows that the first time was only a three-week stint; this time he will be gone for four months, and she is not sure that he will feel the same way about her for the entire duration of his stay. He assures her that he will and proceeds to tell her firmly that there are times when she must be able to let go of the past; she must realize that mistakes will always be made in a long relationship, and although it is important for them to reflect upon their mistakes and to use them to understand and deal with current situations, it is wrong to allow their mistakes to control their opinions of each other.

Allison pauses for a moment, then nods in agreement. She apologizes for not having trusted him, and she tells him that she would never have forgiven herself had she prevented him from going to Milan. After a long hug, they bid farewell to their spot, somehow sensing that it will not be the last time they come there.

Len and Cecilia

Len's girlfriend, Cecilia, has been in South America for almost six months. An archaeologist by trade, Cecilia is currently working on a major project concerning early Inca civilization. She should be home shortly, but nothing is for certain. Before Cecilia went away to South America, she and Len were planning on getting married by the end of the year. Her departure led to a considerable amount of strife; Len understood that the Inca project was a great opportunity for Cecilia, but he felt that there would be others like it in the future and that getting married should be their first priority. Cecilia, however, insisted that there would be other projects for her only if she took advantage of opportunities like this one. She recognized that it would be difficult for Len to be alone for such a long time, but told him that they would get married the moment she got home. Len finally realized that Cecilia was not going to change her mind and decided to stop arguing with her so that at least they could part happily.

The past six months have indeed been difficult for Len. The only way that he has been able to avoid the pangs of loneliness—other than the occasional letter he receives from Cecilia (there are no phones where she is staying)—is to sift through the boxes of photographs that form a record of the times he and Cecilia have shared. The pictures serve not only as physical reminders of the past, but also as mental and emotional reminders. For Len, every picture tells a story of the characters it portrays, replete with their thoughts and feelings. Len has always felt that he and Cecilia should keep a record of their time together. He believes that such a record enables them to gain a better perspective on their relationship, by allowing them to understand their current situation in terms of the past.

Len has just spotted a picture of Cecilia with her best friend, Melissa. He shakes his head slightly, remembering an event that almost ended his relationship with Cecilia. A few years ago, he and Cecilia had accompanied Melissa to an extravagant Fourth of July party. Both Len and Melissa were drinking heavily, but Cecilia was not in a festive mood; before too long, she told them that she was going home. After she left, Len and Melissa started kissing each other. Moments later, Cecilia walked in on them; she had realized that Len and Melissa would need a ride and decided to come back to offer them one. Needless to say, she was devastated by what she saw. Len and Melissa explained that it was nothing serious; they were drunk and were just being silly. Cecilia knew that what they were saying was probably true, but she was nevertheless deeply hurt by the whole incident. She considered ending her relationship with Len but eventually decided that it would be wrong to let one foolish act on his part end the strong bond that they shared. As Len recalls this entire episode today, he sees that he, too, must be able to see beyond Cecilia's decision to go to South America. After all, if she could forgive him for what he had done, he must certainly forgive her for something much more innocuous.

Len takes out another photograph. It is a snapshot of him and Cecilia standing at the rim of the Grand Canyon. They had just spent the entire day walking up from the bottom, and they were thoroughly exhausted. Len fondly recalls the wonderful feeling that he had at the moment the picture was taken. Granted, he was tired, but he felt exhilarated to have climbed to the top, and was even happier because Cecilia was there with him. He remembers thinking how he wanted to spend the rest of his life with her. Looking at this photograph now, he realizes that it is memories like these that have made the past six months bearable.

Modes of Thought and Behavior

The historian thinks a lot about both the events of the past and the continuities and discontinuities between the past and the present. In a relationship, this sense of history can be important.

The stories of Allison and Eric and of Len and Cecilia show how history can both enhance and compromise the prospects of a relationship. In both cases, some of the past memories are of very happy times and help the couples get through difficult times in the present. Because every serious relationship goes through difficult times, having good memories to draw on can be important. At times, those memories may be literally what keeps the couple together. In these cases, the couple can anticipate, or at least hope, that the future will bring more of the happy moments that they have had in the past.

The downside of memories is that when they are bad, they can continue to exert a toxic effect on a relationship years after the event that generated them has supposedly been resolved and put into perspective. Many of us have been with people who won't let go of what they perceive as a mistake or a sin on the part of their partner. No matter how many times the issue seems to have been resolved, it manages to come up again and again. No matter what one tries to do, the partner is unwilling to lay the old issue to rest. Often, the memory is used as a manipulation to get behavioral compliance: "Because of what you did to me in the past, you still owe me, and I can do whatever I want in the present." Such permanent records are toxic not because they are necessarily incorrect, but because they leave the accused partner with no incentive to learn from mistakes. After all, once the mistake is made, it is as though it has been made forever and for always.

Historians know that what makes a history is not simply a record of past events. Instead, history resides in the selection, interpretation, and integrative analysis of these events. Similarly, in relationships, it is not so much what has happened but what has been learned from what has happened that can either help to make or help to break a relationship. Couples who learn from their histories grow in their relationship; those who do not, stagnate or regress.

Complementary Roles: Historians, or Historian and Historical Personage

Typically, individuals with a history story seek out other individuals for whom history is important. They may therefore create a shared history.

Sometimes one person serves as the historian and the other as the historical personage. In such relationships there is a natural asymmetry; indeed, some of the elements of asymmetrical stories (see page 49) may come into play. The historical personage is likely to be the person who is somehow viewed as more important in the relationship. This importance may derive from the significance the partners assign to this person's family background, accomplishments, or life path.

The role of history can change over time in a relationship. For example, when a couple first gets together, they may have a historical bent, going over in endless detail the histories of their lives. They may share, often intimately, what they have learned from mistakes in previous relationships. But once the relationship gets under way, one or both members of the relationship may find themselves much less eager to think and talk about the more recent (and therefore less historical) mistakes of the current relationship. As a result, intimate discussions of what has been learned from one's failures and mistakes may disappear. The cost, of course, is that the couple may not adequately deal with the mistakes they have made, leading to unresolved tensions and hostilities.

Other couples may become more historical over time, especially if children are born. Sometimes it is the birth of children that makes the couple realize that someday they will want a record of all the growth and development that has taken place in their family unit. The couple may therefore start becoming more historically oriented.

Advantages and Disadvantages

The greatest advantage of the history story is the potential for remembering happy moments and for using these moments to get through rough times. The history story also can be helpful in placing in a larger context what seem at the time to be major catastrophes, allowing the partners to realize that an apparently disastrous event later often ceases to seem so important, or even to have any importance at all.

The greatest disadvantage of the history story is the potential for repeatedly dragging up past failures. The individual with this tendency rarely forgets anything and is often ready to bring up an issue from the past, ensuring that the conflict will be reexperienced again and again.

Relationships in which people are unable to forgive, whether or not they forget, tend to be fraught with anxieties and feelings of guilt. It's hard to be happy if any past sin can be instantly replayed at a moment's notice.

THE SCIENCE STORY

People who hold a science story believe that love in general can and should be understood, analyzed, and dissected much like any other natural phenomenon. This belief carries over into the day-to-day aspects of their relationship, so that they tend to be highly analytical of many things (perhaps of almost everything) that happens in the relationship. They are likely, as a result, to spend a fair amount of time explaining to themselves or to their partner what they perceive is going on at a deeper level. This behavior can be functional unless it reaches the point where the analyzer talks but does not listen, or actually interferes with the relationship by overanalyzing it.

The latter effect shows a kind of Heisenberg uncertainty principle as applied to close relationships, where the very act of observing the relationship changes it. For example, analyzing lovemaking while it is in progress is extremely likely to affect the lovemaking, even if that is not the intention of the analyzer.

Diagnosing the Science Story

1 I believe understanding a love relationship is like understanding any other natu phenomenon; you need to uncover its governing rules.

2 I believe that to understand a love relationship, you need to try to study it from scientific perspective.

3 I like to analyze different aspects of my relationship, and I find it quite useful to so.

4 I believe the best way to succeed in a relationship is to approach relationship problems from a logical and scientific point of view.

5 I believe more people could have successful relationships if they approached th relationship problems from a logical perspective rather than an emotional one.

6 I like to sit back and objectively analyze and discuss different aspects of my relationship with my partner.

7 I believe relationships can be optimized by rational analysis and dissection.

8 It is possible for me to analyze and understand my partner pretty much completely.

Alisa and Gary

Alisa believes that she has a fairly comprehensive understanding of intimate relationships. She believes that love can be dissected and analyzed just like any other natural phenomenon.

Whenever Alisa confronts a relationship—whether her own or someone else's—she is quick to analyze it. Gary, a chemical engineer and Alisa's husband of eighteen years, has mixed opinions about his wife's scientific approach to relationships. He is fascinated by her knowledge and understanding of intimate relationships. Although he occasionally is skeptical of her intricate analyses, he often finds himself agreeing with her. After all, he agrees with his wife that much of human behavior, and many human emotions, including love, can be analyzed scientifically.

Gary has a different opinion, however, when he becomes the object of analysis. As with Alisa's interpretations of other people, Gary is stimulated by her intricate and perceptive account of his mind and of his behavior, but he sometimes wishes that Alisa would not be so quick to analyze so much of his behavior and emotions. Indeed, Alisa seems to believe that she can virtually always predict how Gary is going to respond to particular behavior on her part, and she uses this presumed knowledge to handle various situations. There are times when Gary becomes quite defensive in response to Alisa's analyses, especially when she concludes by asserting something about him that he does not believe is true.

Moreover, even when Gary does agree with Alisa's analysis, he still wishes that she would not always be so cerebral in her approach to him and to their relationship. Gary believes that Alisa's approach often lacks romance, which by its very nature involves a great deal of surprise and unpredictability—things a scientific approach does not take into account.

Nevertheless, despite the problems that Gary has with some of the aspects of Alisa's analytic approach to their relationship, he still finds that there are many positive aspects to it. For one, in trying to figure out how he is going to respond to the different things that she says or does, he demonstrates an interest in both Alisa and in the relationship. Moreover, Alisa's scientific approach seems to Gary to be quite effective when it comes to understanding and interpreting the problems that he and Alisa face in their relationship, helping them to arrive at an appropriate solution that is best for both of them.

Colin and Anita

Colin has been interested in science for as long as he can remember. When he was in high school, he used to conduct experiments in his backyard. In college, he pursued a double major in physics and chemistry. Now he is a physics professor at a major university. Colin's interest in science, however, does not stop at the classroom. He believes that the laws of nature apply to people in many of the same ways that they apply to objects. As a result, when he interacts with others, he constantly tries to come up with a scientific, causal analysis of their behavior. In his intimate relationships, Colin is especially determined to understand his partner's behavior. He believes that love can be broken down and understood piece by piece, to the point where he can precisely figure out how his partner is going to respond to various actions, emotions, and circumstances. He tries to learn how his partner is going to react to certain situations, and then he tries to use this information to act appropriately in the future.

At first it might appear as though Colin's scientific approach to intimate relationships is very impersonal. However, although his attitude is rather scientific, there is also a personal quality to it: The scientific approach is distinctively Colin's. Most important, the primary reason Colin seeks to understand his partner is to get to know her better as a person. He wants to come to an understanding of her wants and her needs. Moreover, his analysis is intended to make his relationship work as well as it possibly can.

For the most part, Colin's current girlfriend, Anita, does not mind Colin's analytic approach to their relationship. In fact, she believes that there are many advantages to such an approach. For one, it shows that he is interested both in getting to know her better and in coming to a more nearly complete understanding of their relationship. In addition, because Colin's scientific approach emphasizes the importance of taking every side of an issue into consideration, she feels it is helpful when it comes to solving many of the problems that she and Colin face, for she knows he will listen to her point of view. At times, however, Anita wishes that Colin would not always intellectualize their relationship. She understands that Colin's approach reflects his personality, but now and then she feels like a rat in a maze. Nevertheless, she understands that Colin really does care for her, and although his approach to their relationship might seem impersonal, she knows that for him it is not.

Modes of Thought and Behavior

A person with a science story believes that love can be understood through analysis and dissection. The person is likely to believe in his or her ability not only to understand but to predict and even control the behavior of the partner. The scientist watches rather carefully for regularities in the behavior of self and others and seeks to make generalizations based on them.

Scientists differ in their objectivity, both with respect to others and with respect to themselves. This point underscores the fact that someone's being a scientist in no way ensures that they will do good science. A scientist can analyze other people's behavior all day, yet be wrong in every analysis he or she makes. The role of scientist only ensures the existence of an interest in scientific analysis, not the quality of that analysis.

Some individuals, like Colin, work in the sciences and attempt to apply a scientific approach in almost every aspect of their lives. Other individuals, like Alisa, are scientific with respect to intimate relationships, but don't really care much about actual science in other aspects of their lives.

There are several important points to recognize with regard to this science story. First, a person who can successfully apply scientific analysis in one domain (say, biology or physics) does not necessarily apply it equally successfully in another domain.[1] Thus, the fact that someone is a successful scientist on the job does not mean that this person will be a successful scientist in his or her intimate relationships.

Second, people may be successful as scientists in their analyses of the relationships of others, but not in the analysis of their own relationships. A distinction is sometimes made between interpersonal intelligence and intrapersonal intelligence, the former meaning intelligence in one's relationships with others, and the latter meaning intelligence in one's relationship with oneself.[2] The two kinds of intelligence show very little relationship to each other, so that the fact that one can successfully analyze others' behavior does not imply that one will successfully analyze one's own behavior, and vice versa.

Indeed, psychotherapists have much the same problems in their relationships that other people have in theirs.

Third, we all analyze our relationships to some degree, but relatively few people have a science story. The science story comes into play when a person dwells on analysis and is rarely content just to let things be. Scientists are not truly happy in relationships unless they feel they understand them. Thus, for scientists, understanding does not follow from or after happiness, but rather is a principal part of it.

Complementary Roles: Scientist and Object of Study

The two complementary roles in the science story are typically the scientist and someone else, who, along with the relationship, form the object of study. Sometimes, but not often, both partners are scientists. Such relationships can be difficult unless the two scientists bring the same worldview to their analyses.

Advantages and Disadvantages

The greatest advantage of the science story is that it may truly lead to insights about a relationship and the partners in it and, in the ideal case, positive behavioral change. Many couples fail to improve their relationships because they are unaware of what it is that needs to be improved. A scientist will hypothesize about the strengths and weaknesses of the relationship, thus opening the way to constructive change.

One of the potential downsides of the science story, however, is the possibility that the analysis is incorrect, which can lead to friction and behavioral change that actually worsens rather than improves a relationship. People in a relationship with a scientist also may resent the analysis, or believe that they deserve better than to be treated as an object of study.

Another potential downside is that the analysis will alter the relationship and result in a loss of the spontaneity that is part of almost any good relationship. When people feel that they are constantly being analyzed, they just don't behave the same way they would otherwise. They are also likely to become resentful. Thus, partners in such a relationship need to find ways of keeping the analyzing from getting out of hand.

☞ THE COOKBOOK STORY

The cookbook story is characterized by the view that if two people in a close relationship do things in a certain way—that is, if they follow a recipe—the relationship is almost certain to work out. In this story, relationships succeed because they follow certain, fixed steps, and the key is to figure out what these steps are, what order to enact them in, and how to enact them effectively.

This story is the one that fuels much of the market for popular books on how to make relationships work. The problem, of course, is that these books are likely to work effectively only for those who hold a cookbook story. For some such individuals, the exact steps of the recipe may matter less than that they have some set of steps to follow. But for other individuals, recipes just do not work, perhaps as shown by the fact that the average shelf life of self-help books on relationships tends to be mercifully short. The books disappear, but soon are replaced by new books making the same claims, perhaps even more strongly.

Diagnosing the Cookbook Story

1 I believe there is a right way and a wrong way of approaching close relationships. You can succeed if you know the right way.
2 I believe that to have a good relationship you need to follow all the necessary steps one by one.
3 I believe the recipe for a great relationship is like the recipe for a great dish; it requires the right ingredients and attention to details.
4 I believe that those who have succeeded in their relationships are those who have discovered what it takes to do them just right.

5 I believe that being successful in one's close relationship is like being able to ⟨⟩ well; using too much or too little of the necessary ingredients may prove disastrous.

6 I believe a good relationship must follow certain steps to success.

7 I believe making a relationship work is much like following a recipe for succe⟨⟩ cooking.

8 I believe there is a recipe for success in relationships that some people find an⟨⟩ others don't.

Fred and Pauline

Neither Fred nor Pauline plans to get married anytime soon; they are both coming off of rough divorces, and they do not want to rush into anything. Nevertheless, they hope to have a long, fulfilling relationship with each other. Of course, if things go well, marriage would certainly not be out of the question.

In order to make their relationship last, Fred and Pauline know that they must both be happy with the time they spend together. They recognize that finding happiness will not be easy for them. Fred loves playing and watching sports, whereas Pauline is more interested in going out dancing and watching movies. In an effort to get beyond this problem, they have decided to implement a system whereby they both get to do what they want. To appease Fred, they will go running together twice a week, and will attend at least one sporting event every month; to make Pauline happy, they will go to a movie once a week, and will go out dancing every other week. They also have agreed to handle all other disputes regarding how they should spend their time together in a similar fashion—that is, by reaching a compromise. Both Pauline and Fred believe that if they stick to this formula, they will have a successful relationship.

Several months go by, and it appears as though Pauline and Fred were right about their prediction. They have assiduously followed their formula for success, and they are both having a great time. Pauline has even started to like running, and for the first time in her life, she shouted during a baseball game a couple of weeks ago. As for Fred, he has picked up some pretty impressive dance moves and has become a self-proclaimed movie critic. Pauline has decided to move in with Fred, and although they had both determined to wait a considerable amount of time before even thinking about marriage, both can sense that wedding bells might not be too far off.

Fred and Pauline understand that they cannot become too rigid with their recipe for success. They recognize that no one formula can guarantee a successful relationship and that they must be willing to modify their activities if various circumstances demand that they do so. For instance, with winter approaching, Fred realizes that there will be days when it will be impossible for him and Pauline to go running. Likewise, Pauline knows that there will be nights when Fred simply will not want to go dancing. Fred and Pauline agree that when such circumstances arise, they will try to come up with new activities to satisfy their respective needs. They believe that as long as they continue to make compromises, their relationship most likely will remain a successful one.

Elizabeth and Isaac

Every Thursday night at six, Elizabeth and Isaac convene at Isaac's apartment for dinner and a movie. The meal they prepare for themselves is usually an elaborate affair, with a fresh salad, a couple of appetizers, and a delicious main course. After they finish eating, they walk to the video store and pick out a movie that neither of them has seen. On the way back, they stop off at the supermarket and buy a small carton of ice cream to share during the movie. When they return to Isaac's place, they put the video in the VCR, flip off the lights, and cuddle up together under their favorite blanket, wrapping themselves in each other's arms.

Not everything in Isaac and Elizabeth's relationship is as romantic and idyllic as their Thursday night ritual. In fact, the activities of that particular evening are just about the only things that Isaac and Elizabeth can agree upon. For the most part, their tastes are entirely different: Isaac enjoys listening to independent rock bands in some of the downtown clubs; Elizabeth likes to go browsing in antiquarian bookstores. Elizabeth finds the music that Isaac listens to unbearable; Isaac believes there could be nothing more boring than spending an entire day looking through musty books. Because of their busy work schedules and conflicting interests, Isaac and Elizabeth have less time together than they would like. As a result, at Elizabeth's urging, they make certain to spend whatever spare time they do have engaging in an activity that appeals to both of them. Hence, they try to make their Thursday night ritual as romantic and as enjoyable as possible. Of course, they do not just spend Thursday evening together, but it is the one time that they are sure to be with each other. They believe that as long as they have this one special night each week, they will be able to maintain a successful relationship despite their differences.

Despite their optimism, Elizabeth and Isaac both recognize that they cannot be too rigid with their Thursday night ritual. They understand that it is foolish to think that any one formula will guarantee success. Elizabeth has several times expressed her concern that there may come a time when the combination of dinner, ice cream, and a movie will no longer work out for them as well as it does now. If such a time comes, Elizabeth and Isaac know, they will have to modify their Thursday night ritual, or perhaps even find other activities that also appeal to them. The important thing is that they find a recipe upon which they both can agree, and that they be willing to alter the recipe if it becomes necessary to do so. Elizabeth and Isaac believe that if they continue to stick to these principles, their relationship will remain a successful one.

Modes of Thought and Behavior

The cookbook story is an exceedingly popular one, as shown by the market for pop psychology books. Indeed, we are often brought up believing that there should be a "right" way to run a relationship, and hence that our problem is to figure out what this "right" way is.

Psychologists often distinguish between "well-structured problems" and "ill-structured problems."[1] The difference between the two is that well-structured problems have a clear and correct path to a solution, whereas ill-structured problems do not. For example, an algebra word problem would be a well-structured problem, whereas the problem of how to argue persuasively in favor of a political position would be an ill-structured problem. Recipes such as those found in pop psychology books for improving relationships assume that the problem of how to form a loving relationship is a well-structured problem. For some, like Fred and Pauline, and Elizabeth and Isaac, it is, because of their cookbook stories. For most people, though, it isn't.

Why would people believe that a problem is well structured if it isn't? There are many reasons. For one, we are taught almost from the time we are in first grade that problems not only are but should be well structured. Textbooks tend to present problems authoritatively, with right and wrong answers. Many of the tests we take have questions with right and wrong answers. Religion may teach us that there are right and wrong answers. Politicians imply that there are such answers (and, of course, that they have them, and that their opponents only claim to). There are plenty of forces in our environment to socialize us into believing that life's problems should have a single right answer, whether they do or not.[2] It should therefore not be surprising that the cookbook story is a popular one.

Whether people believe that such right answers exist also depends on their style of thinking.[3] I have proposed elsewhere a theory about styles of thinking, according to which, for example, some people prefer to independently arrive at a solution to their problem, whereas other people prefer to be told what to do. Many couples with cookbook stories prefer to be told what to do and, once having decided on a course of action, want to keep doing the same thing over and over again.

But there are also couples, like Elizabeth and Isaac, who basically make their own recipe. Once the recipe is in place, however, they may be as rigid in following it as other couples would be who take their recipes from others. Probably the most successful "cookbook couples" are those who are flexible, changing the recipe over time and when they enter into a new relationship.

Complementary Roles: Cooks, Chefs, Chef and Cook

The two principal complementary roles always involve two people working together to prepare a dish (their relationship) based on a recipe. What differs across relationships is what the recipe is and where it originates. Cooks take their recipes from the outside; chefs make up their own recipes. In the case of a chef and a cook, one person takes most of the responsibility for coming up with the recipe, the other for actually cooking it up.

In cook-cook relationships, both partners take their direction from outside. They are likely to be people who read self-help books, watch television shows about intimate partnerships, or listen to radio shows discussing what constitutes a good relationship. Or they may take their direction from having watched their parents and other couples.

Chef-cook relationships can work out quite well, because the responsibilities are clearly distributed: One person is responsible primarily for coming up with the recipe, the other for making the recipe work. Elizabeth and Isaac have this kind of relationship, with Elizabeth taking the role of the chef. If we look at their thinking styles, we see that one individual likes to decide what to do, whereas the other generally likes to be told what to do. The greatest risk factor for this kind of relationship is that the chef will become bored with the cook, because the chef is the one who tends to come up with the ideas, or that the cook will start to resent the chef's always being the one to decide on the recipe the partners should follow.

A third possibility is a chef-chef relationship, such as Fred and Pauline have. Both take roughly equal responsibility for deciding on their own personal recipe. Such relationships are more egalitarian than chef-cook relationships in their distribution of responsibilities. As in the cook-cook relationship, both people take on the same role. There is greater potential for conflict in this kind of relationship, however, if the two partners cannot agree on a recipe. In such cases, they either will need good conflict resolution strategies or will need to find another relationship in which the recipes are more nearly compatible.

Advantages and Disadvantages

Cookbook stories have as their greatest advantage the idea that there is a more or less well-defined strategy for making the relationship work, and it often is even out in the open, as in the cases of Fred and Pauline and of Elizabeth and Isaac. People know what they are supposed to do and usually whether they are doing it.

There is also a kind of idealism about this kind of relationship that can give people hope: Even if they have not found the right recipe, there is always the possibility they will. Thus, some couples with this story who feel that things are not working out as well as they should in the relationship are willing to invest in counseling, weekend retreats, courses, or whatever else it takes to find the right recipe. In a way, some couples with this kind of idealism resemble optimistic dieters who are constantly searching for the diet that will work for them, but seem never quite to find it. They are always eager to buy the next diet book to hit the bookstores, in the hope that this diet, unlike all the others, will provide them with the recipe for permanent weight loss. Some people find such a recipe; more do not.

The greatest potential disadvantage of the cookbook story is rigidity: The couple gets locked into a recipe that does not work for them, or one that once worked for them but that is no longer working. Cookbook stories probably have their greatest success when the partners are flexible in the creation and implementation of their recipes.

Another potential disadvantage, as implied above, is not knowing when to quit. Suppose that two partners are in a relationship that is not working out well, and so they go to counseling. The counseling doesn't help. Thinking that maybe the counselor wasn't so great, they go to another counselor. She or he doesn't help, either. Well, can the couple ever be sure that counseling can't work, that it is a bound to be a total flop—an utter failure? No, because no matter how many counselors they go to without a successful outcome, it is always possible that the next one will yield a successful outcome. It may be the third, the fifth, or the hundred-and-seventeenth, but no matter how many failures there are, there is always hope. Those with a cookbook story, though, need to take responsibility for deciding when this hope is as elusive as a particular grain of sand on a beach—when, for them, there is simply no viable recipe to be found.

GENRE STORIES

I n genre stories, the mode or way of being in the relationship is key to the existence and maintenance of the relationship. Some special ongoing feature of the relationship dominates other aspects of it. In a war story, an ongoing war and the many battles to which it gives rise dominate the relationship; the war is never won or lost, because for the relationship to survive as a war story, the war must be unending. In a theater story, one partner (or sometimes both partners) engage(s) in a role. The relationship is like theater. The role or roles may change, but the theatrical aspect never does. In a humor story, jokes, lightheartedness, and seeing the funny side of things predominate. Any attempt at a serious or even conflictual conversation is likely to be diverted by humor. In a mystery story, one of the partners seems continually to be shrouded in a cloak of mystery, and the relationship evolves as the other partner tries, never completely successfully, to penetrate the shroud. Usually, as soon as one shroud is penetrated, another quickly takes its place.

⇌ THE WAR STORY

In a war story, a couple views love as a series of battles in a war—often, a prolonged and devastating war. The curious thing is that if both partners have this view, they may be quite happy in what appears to others to be an awful relationship.

193

Just as some people become warriors by profession, some couples are warriors in their relationships, and truly are at their happiest when they are fighting what they see as the good fight. Were the fight to end, the couple, like warriors at the end of a war, might find themselves not quite sure what to do with themselves. If, however, only one member of a couple has a war story, what is quite acceptable for one partner may be hell for the other.

Diagnosing the War Story

1   I think arguing is healthy for a close relationship.
2   I think fights actually make a relationship more vital.
3   I think relationships in which partners do not have frequent arguments are dead.
4   I think it is more interesting to argue than to compromise.
5   I think frequent arguments help bring conflictive issues into the open and keep th relationship healthy.
6   I enjoy battling a lot with my partner to keep things interesting.
7   Relationships involve a great deal of conflict, which I believe is actually good for the relationship.
8   I actually like to fight with my partner.

Bob and Dierdre

It is the same old story for Bob and Dierdre. Sitting at the dinner table, Bob asks his wife, Dierdre, if she has reconsidered her decision to keep their son in public school. Dierdre closes her eyes and takes a deep breath, trying her best to remain calm. The couple has been arguing for weeks about whether or not to keep John in public school, and after several horrible fights Dierdre finally thought that she and Bob had come to an agreement. However, she now senses that a new fight is brewing, and realizes that the issue is not yet settled.

Bob has seen this expression on Dierdre's face before, and knows how to interpret it. Immediately he accuses her of acting condescendingly toward him; he maintains that his opinions are as important as hers are, and that she must acknowledge this fact. She agrees with him but maintains that the decision to keep John in public school has nothing to do with their opinions; the only thing that matters is what is best for their son. At this, Bob slams his fist on the table and asks his wife if she thinks it is best for their son to have to confront gangs and drugs every day of his life for the next four years. He starts screaming at her, and Dierdre can only shake her head as her son storms up to his room.

Shouting matches like this one between Bob and Dierdre have been going on for almost fifteen years. Dierdre swore she would try to keep the marriage together until after John finished high school, although she does not know how many more battles she can fight with her husband. Bob has always felt that one should fight for what one believes in, and family matters have never been an exception. Dierdre has always preferred a more sedate way of discussing issues; ironically, though, over the years she has found that the only way she can tolerate the fighting is to adopt Bob's view about it and battle with him every step of the way. Otherwise, in order to avoid Bob's rage, she will usually cave in to whatever he wants. Unfortunately, she has noticed that when she reciprocates Bob's behavior, it has a worse effect on John, and so she tries to avoid fighting with her husband whenever possible. However, she considers the school issue to be a very important one; after discussing it with friends, relatives, and even teachers and principals from both public and private schools, she feels public school would be the better choice for her son. Therefore she believes that she must combat her husband at every turn.

John's schooling is an important issue, and fighting over it may be inevitable, but the issues over which Bob and Dierdre engage in battle are not always of this magnitude. Just last week they had a dispute over whether or not to keep the living room couch. Bob thought it was old and filthy; Dierdre thought it had a lot of charm. Bob began to accuse Dierdre of being a slob and setting a poor example for John. They had just finished arguing about where John should go to school, and so Dierdre could not believe that a fight was starting up again, especially one of such a trivial nature.

Nevertheless, Dierdre recognizes that their relationship always has been and probably always will be characterized by continuous strife, and that no matter what the issue, a fight will probably always be just right around the corner.

Natasha and Marcus

It is late in the fourth quarter of the big Monday night game between the Pittsburgh Steelers and the Kansas City Chiefs. Marcus, a huge Steelers fan, is pacing anxiously across the room as he watches his team march down the field in quest of a go-ahead touchdown.

Natasha, Marcus's girlfriend for the past two years, storms into the room and asks him if the game is ever going to end. Marcus, too absorbed in the game to hear what Natasha is saying, gives her a cursory wave of his hand to indicate that he wants to be left alone. Natasha whispers angrily under her breath that she will not tolerate this ridiculous behavior any longer, and then proceeds to walk directly in front of the television. His eyes widening in agony, Marcus places one hand on each side of his head and lets out a loud scream. Natasha retaliates by yelling out how absurd it is that he cares more about a stupid football team than about the promotion that she has just been given. Marcus, trying to remain calm, tells her that they will celebrate her promotion tomorrow; he then pleads with her to let him watch the final minutes of the game in peace. In response, Natasha furiously walks out of the room, ripping down one of Marcus's Steelers posters as she exits.

A few minutes later the Steelers win in dramatic fashion, but Marcus's celebration is cut short when Natasha returns to the room and continues her verbal assault on him. Marcus tries to get her to relax, but he knows by now that once she starts, it is almost impossible for her to stop. He explains to her, as he has many times before, that he recognizes the absurdity and irrationality of his passion for the Steelers; he maintains, however, that it is hardly a criminal offense, and that she should be considerate enough to leave him alone for the three hours a week that the Steelers play. Natasha replies that her state of mind has nothing to do with how much time Marcus spends watching the Steelers; rather, it is the principle of the whole thing that makes her so angry—the idea that he cares more about the Steelers than about her.

Marcus begins to respond, but she will hear nothing of it; she leaves the room and goes straight to the bedroom, locking the door after she walks in. Marcus sits down on the couch and puts his head in his hands. This scene has become a much too common occurrence in his relationship with Natasha; if it isn't the Steelers, it's something else. Whatever the topic, Natasha is always willing to fight for what she believes is right, and she will continue to argue until Marcus gives in to her; if he does not do so, she will simply walk away and refuse to talk to him.

As Marcus broods over his relationship, Natasha storms back into the room. She tells him in a rather cruel voice that she is going to inform her boss that she no longer needs his box seat ticket to the next Steelers game, which she had promised to get for Marcus. For a moment Marcus's heart almost stops, but he gathers himself and just shakes his head.

Modes of Thought and Behavior

The primary mode of thought in the war story is that love is war—that a good relationship is about fighting. People with this story feel that they must be ready to fight for what they believe is right. What is more, the need for a battle arises fairly predictably, for their partner holds an opposing view on whatever topic is in contention.

For those who do not have a war story, it can seem incredible that anyone would. Why would anyone *want* to fight? After all, conflict is associated with the dissolution, not the construction, of relationships.[1] But asking this question is like asking why anyone would want to join the army or the navy. For people who are warriors, the satisfaction is in the good fight. And for those with a war story, the good fight (and sometimes a dirty one) is what relationships are all about.

Complementary Roles: Conquering Warriors and Vanquished Warriors

In a successful war story, both partners are warriors, and there will be many skirmishes as well as some major battles, each with a winner and a loser—a conqueror and the vanquished. For couples in this kind of relationship, much of the enjoyment is in being the conqueror as much of the time as possible; but when a battle is lost, there is always the next battle to look forward to, and the possibility of recouping what was lost in the last one.

Advantages and Disadvantages

This story is advantageous in a relationship only when both partners clearly share it and want the same thing. In these cases, threats of divorce and worse may be common, but neither partner would seriously dream of leaving: They're both having too much fun, in their own way. The major disadvantage, of course, is that the story often isn't shared, leading to intense and sustained conflict that can leave the partner without the war story feeling devastated much of the time.

People can find themselves in a warring relationship without either of them having war as a preferred story. In such cases, the constant fighting may be of a kind that makes both partners miserable. If the war continues in such a context, there is no joy in it for either partner.

☞ THE THEATER STORY

In the theater story, one or both partners see themselves as acting out parts. Love follows one of a number of scripts, often with highly structured lines, scenes, and acts.[1] The partner's behavior may be histrionic or it may be flat, but once the scene has been set, it is predictable.

In some relationships based on the theater story, partners know what they are getting into and are satisfied with it. In other cases, though, one partner discovers only after the relationship has formed that the way the other person is acting with them follows a sort of script—emotions or behavior that appear to be genuine are in fact artificial and have been gone through many times before, perhaps without regard to who is serving as the audience of the moment.

Diagnosing the Theater Story

ACTOR
1 I think my relationships are like plays; some are comedies, some are dramas.
2 I frequently put on an act for my partner.
3 I often find myself playing a role in my relationship, just like in a play.
4 I think of my relationship as acting in a play, except that I create my own unique surprise ending.

FAN
1 I often find myself attracted to partners who are able to play different roles, like actors in a play.
2 I like partners who can play different roles from one minute to the next.
3 I like partners who have a sense of drama about themselves, like actors in a play.
4 I enjoy dating partners who are able to change their behavior according to the occasion, just like actors in a play.

Robert and Cindy

Everyone keeps telling Robert how much he is going to like his sister's new roommate, Cindy. Tonight she is throwing a party, and Robert is eager to see if he likes her as much as everyone says he will. Robert spends several hours preparing himself for the evening; in case he falls for Cindy, he wants to make sure not only that he looks good, but that he has a wide array of effective lines and conversation topics to choose from. Reflecting on previous experiences, Robert knows that the difference between success and failure could come down to something as simple as the delivery of a particular line or the amount of emotion he conveys while looking into her eyes.

Fully prepared, Robert walks up to his sister's apartment and rings the doorbell. A beautiful woman opens the door and introduces herself as Cindy. Robert is extremely attracted to her, but he makes sure not to act too interested right away; he shakes her hand politely and then immediately moves on to say hello to his sister. He knows that if he shows too much interest early on, Cindy will be turned off; after all, nobody wants anything that can be had so easily. Robert talks with several people at the party, all the while keeping track of where Cindy is. He wants to be certain that whenever he makes someone laugh, she will be able to witness it.

As the evening progresses, Robert starts making eye contact with Cindy. He has been aloof for long enough; it's now time to let her know that he is interested in her. When the party begins to wind down, he moves over toward her and strikes up a conversation. He starts talking about how strange life is, with its almost random sequence of emotions and events. He can tell she is intrigued, and he uses her interest to feed his theatrical fervor. A few minutes later everyone else has left, and Robert's sister tells them that she is going to bed.

Seizing the opportunity, Robert decides subtly to transform the conversation into a discussion about relationships. During an awkward moment of silence, he summons up his best James Dean impersonation and tells her in a soft voice that he thinks he might really like her. He then tells her that he must get going, but that he would love to have dinner with her sometime. She agrees, and before he gets up to leave, he gives her a soft kiss on the lips.

Two nights later Robert and Cindy are on their first date. Just as on the night they met, Robert is putting on quite a show. He tells funny stories and gives complex psychological interpretations of couples who are sitting near their table—all the while paying close attention to how Cindy responds, so as to determine what his next act should be. At this point, it appears that Robert can do no wrong. Cindy is having a wonderful time. If anything, she thinks Robert is too perfect; there must be a catch.

As the weeks go by, Cindy begins to wonder if perhaps Robert has put on the same show for someone in the past. There are times when she thinks he simply has a vibrant, theatrical personality; there are other times, however, when it seems as if he is just following some scripted formula. For instance, one day she found a container of Pez candy, with a red ribbon around it, in her purse. Robert had obviously put it there, and at first she thought it was really sweet, but while talking to him about it on the phone, she noticed Robert's sister shaking her head with a slight grin, as if to say, "The old Pez-in-the-purse thing, huh?" Cindy would obviously find it distressing if Robert's humor and romantic gestures were just part of an act he has put on for countless other women before her. But are they?

Kellen and Peter

As Peter walks into the Wayfarer, a local bar, he immediately fixes his eyes on the woman standing by the pool table. In her left hand she is elegantly holding a cigarette; when she smokes it, she inhales slowly and exhales gracefully, separating her lips only slightly to prevent the smoke from rushing out and clouding her face. In her right hand she has what appears to be a margarita; she holds it with two fingers on the bottom and sips it gently through a thin cocktail straw. Her beauty matches her grace, and although Peter would love to talk to her, he feels so undignified in comparison to her and wonders if she would like someone like him. He decides to try it anyway, and casually approaches her.

She does not even glance at him as he walks over. He summons up his courage, however, and asks her name. With a slight, almost condescending grin, she tells him that it is Kellen. Oddly, she does not ask Peter for his name, and he wonders if he should just walk away. Every once in a while, though, she turns to him and gives him a look that seems to indicate that she might like him, and so he decides not to leave.

As the night wears on, Kellen begins to speak to him occasionally, but she nevertheless remains aloof. Although somewhat mystified by it, Peter is actually quite intrigued by Kellen's indifferent attitude toward him. He wonders whether he should ask for her phone number, but before he makes his decision, Kellen takes a piece of paper out of her purse, writes her number on it, and tells Peter to give her a call. He is now more perplexed than ever, but he is nevertheless thrilled with the way that the night turned out.

Peter calls Kellen and they make plans to go out to dinner together. The date goes very well; Kellen's demeanor is as dazzling as it was on the night they met. They arrange to see each other again, and Kellen suggests that they have a picnic by the lake just outside of the city. Peter agrees, and he is already looking forward to the outing. The day of the picnic is a beautiful one, and Peter is almost painfully aroused by Kellen's stunning presence. She carries herself like a movie star, and, at times, Peter wonders if he has been magically inserted into a Hollywood romance; Kellen's every move seems flawless, drawing him almost hypnotically toward her.

Peter starts seeing Kellen on a regular basis, and he is continually astounded by her. In a way, though, he is starting to wonder how it is possible for someone to be so completely composed all of the time. He even thinks of asking her about it, but before he gets a chance, he receives some rather shocking information.

One night, while he is describing Kellen to a friend, someone happens to overhear what he is saying. The eavesdropper, it turns out, had a brief relationship with her, and to the amazement of both of them, it turns out that the outings that Peter has had with Kellen are almost identical to the outings that this person had with her. Everything, from the way she handled the initial scene at the bar to the way she orchestrated their first kiss, was almost exactly the same in both cases. Peter smiles bitterly as he realizes it has all been an act.

Modes of Thought and Behavior

In the theater story, everything seems to go according to script. Everyone, of course, follows scripts to some extent; what distinguishes this story is a matter of degree. In the theater story, almost everything, down to the smallest details of an interaction, is planned as much as possible in advance, not only for effect but for a nonscripted appearance. Most often one partner is unaware that he or she is on the receiving end of stage lines until some time after the relationship has begun. Sometimes the partner never catches on.

To the person who serves as the audience in the theater story, the whole relationship can rather suddenly take on an air of artificiality and hypocrisy. But for the actor, however, scripts are what relationships are about; what the actor is doing is what he or she feels is the proper way a relationship should be handled in order to produce optimal results. Perhaps the individual has had role models who were highly scripted, or perhaps the individual has tried to be spontaneous in the past, failed, and found greater success sticking to prescribed lines. In any case, this individual may not feel hypocritical or artificial at all. In some cases, he or she may not even be consciously aware that a script is being followed.

Complementary Roles: Actor and Audience

The two common roles in the theater story are the actor and the audience. In some cases, both people may be engaged in an act, with each other as the audience.

Advantages and Disadvantages

Theater relationships can succeed when either of the partners is unaware of the scriptedness of the behavior. In many cases, only one person is acting, and the relationship may fail when the other partner discovers that he or she is receiving contrived lines. The relationship may nevertheless succeed if the scriptedness is not conscious and there is no intention to deceive. In this case, success is possible if the person who serves as the audience recognizes that what appears to be an act is just the way the other individual is most comfortable in close relationships.

⌐ THE HUMOR STORY

The humor story tends to be a lighthearted one, in which one or both participants like to see the funny side of things. One or both partners are likely to joke a lot, and the joking can become a ritual. When there is a conflict, the partner or partners may find themselves "solving" it by turning it into a joke—they see the humorous side to it, then move on. People with a humor story are concerned that nothing be taken too seriously in the relationship, and when a conversation is becoming very serious, they may start joking. If their partner does not share a humor story, the partner may find him- or herself taken aback by the seeming inappropriateness of the timing with which jokes seem to arise.

Diagnosing the Humor Story

AUDIENCE
1   I like a partner who is willing to think about the funny side of our conflicts.
2   I like partners who are able occasionally to see the humorous side of issues.
3   I think taking a relationship too seriously can spoil it; that's why I like partners who have a sense of humor.
4   I like a partner who makes me laugh whenever we are facing a tense situation in our relationship.

COMEDIAN
1   I admit that I sometimes try to use humor in order to avoid facing a problem in my relationship.
2   Often I like to joke around when my partner is upset with me, mainly because I think it is healing to be able to laugh at yourself even when you are facing a difficult situation in your relationship.

3　I like to use humor when I have a conflict with my partner because I believe there is always a humorous side to any conflict situation in relationships.

4　When I disagree with my partner, I often try to make a joke out of it.

Dolores and Wally

From the moment Dolores started seeing Wally, she knew that, at the very least, the relationship would contain many laughs. On their first date, they were initially having some difficulty communicating; each of them was asking the other the standard first-date questions, and each, in turn, was receiving the standard first-date answers. Suddenly, in response to the dreary, uninspiring conversation they were having, Wally suggested that they stop having such an enthralling discussion; his brain was experiencing too much stimulation.

It was the perfect line at the time, serving to release the tension of the situation and allow them to get to know each other better. Immediately Wally began pointing out other couples in the restaurant who appeared to be having difficulty communicating, and he started giving humorous, detailed accounts of their relationships. Dolores was in hysterics, and she began her own analysis of several of the couples in the restaurant. Soon both she and Wally were laughing uncontrollably, and stopped their antics only when many people began to look over at them.

Dolores's prediction that she and Wally would share many laughs together has turned out to be true. Their ability to recognize that there is a humorous side to many of the events in their lives has provided them with a lot of fun times, and it has enabled them to get through many awkward moments as well. If there is any problem at all with the relationship, it is that Dolores occasionally worries that Wally is not taking the relationship seriously enough. Ordinarily she joins him in his jocularity regarding their relationship; however, there are times when she wants to be serious, such as when she would like to focus on the long term. Wally often responds to such requests with a joke, one that usually makes fun of either her or the question. There was one time when she asked him if he had considered marrying her; he said he had, on the condition that they would not have to live together. It was obvious that Dolores was not amused; sensing this fact, Wally insisted that he was only kidding, but nevertheless continued to avoid the question. Situations like this one sometimes make Dolores feel that Wally may have a fear of intimacy, and be covering it up with his humorous antics.

The majority of the time, however, Dolores does not question Wally's approach to the relationship. She usually adopts his attitude and plays right along with him. She recognizes that the humor is a central part of the relationship, and that she and Wally truly care about each other. As long as this is the case, she sees no reason to put a stop to the fun that Wally's antics provide.

Nelson and Emily

Emily is at it again. Her boyfriend, Nelson, has just asked her if she has given any thought to whether they should move in together, and, as usual, Emily is busy delivering one funny line after another about the topic, rather than seriously discussing it. She first mentions the bad points of moving in together, such as the various inconveniences that arise when two people of the opposite sex share the same bathroom. Turning to the good points, she facetiously remarks that there is a lesser chance of getting locked out of the apartment if there are two people living in it; she adds that having an extra person in her bed to respond to the alarm clock should make it easier for her to get to work on time. Although Nelson cannot help laughing at some of Emily's remarks, he realizes that this is just her way of evading an important question. He wishes that she would stop trying to be so funny and that she would start being more serious about their relationship.

Emily has always treated both love and relationships in a humorous fashion. She remarks that people never stop to realize how absurd life is and how uncontrollable human behavior and human emotions are; she argues that if they did, they, too, would recognize the importance of laughing at themselves and the relationships in which they get involved. Although Nelson wishes that Emily would not always deal with problematic situations or important decisions by resorting to her humorous approach, he does agree with her viewpoint to a certain extent. Moreover, he believes that there are many advantages to viewing relationships in a humorous manner. In addition to the amusement and all the laughs he gets from listening to Emily's litany of hilarious jokes and witty comments, he feels it is important to recognize that there is a light side to life, especially when everything seems to be going against you. In the same vein, there have been many tense moments that he and Emily have been able to get through because of Emily's ability to find something funny about the situation. For instance, when they were just starting to see one another, they went out one evening and wound up getting extremely drunk. When they woke up in bed together the next morning, neither of them really remembered what had happened. Needless to say, it was a rather awkward moment, and both were wondering if it would mark an end to their recently established relationship. It very well could have, had it not been for Emily's ensuing discussion of inebriated sexual encounters. Her hilarious analysis included a complex diagram, replete with bunny rabbits, the alcoholic dew that the rabbits drink, and, of course, the appropriately furnished rabbit bedroom. When she finished, Nelson probably felt closer to her than he ever had to anyone before; in fact, this episode probably served to solidify their status as a couple.

Modes of Thought and Behavior

A humor story is characterized by the view that love is strange and in many ways funny. We can see either the serious side or the light side of love relationships, and people with a humor story definitely prefer to see the light side. They use humor to create interest for themselves, to defuse conflict, and at times to avoid confronting serious questions and to maintain some degree of distance from their partner.

One of the biggest risk that relationships face is stagnation. People simply become bored. The humor story provides one way to avoid boredom, because the possibilities for new humorous adventures in a relationship are essentially endless. If there is a risk, it is that always seeing the humorous side of things will itself become dull.

Complementary Roles: Comedian and Audience

The two roles in the humor story are the comedian and the audience. These roles may shift between one partner and the other, but at a given time, the comedian needs an audience in order to succeed in his or her role. As we have all discovered at one time or another, funniness, like beauty, is in the mind of the beholder, and a comedian who is not rewarded with appreciation for his or her jokes is likely to stop joking, or, in the case of someone who is drawn to humor as a love story, to leave or distance him- or herself mentally or emotionally from a relationship.

Advantages and Disadvantages

The humor story can have one enormous advantage: Most situations do have a lighter side, and the individual with this story is more likely than others to see it. When things in a relationship become tense or when partners feel that life is weighing them down, sometimes nothing works better than a little humor, especially if it comes from within the relationship rather than from outside it.

Humor stories also allow relationships to be creative and dynamic, and to respond to the joyous side of life's experiences. People can find the humorous aspect to their relationship to be a source of happiness and a constant reminder that there are few things that in the long term end up being as seriously wrong as they may seem at the moment.

The humor story also has some potential disadvantages. Probably the greatest one is the risk of deflecting important issues with humor: A serious conversation that needs to take place—say, between Nelson and Emily about living together—keeps getting put off or deflected by jokes. Thus humor can serve to deflect rather than promote intimacy.[1] Eventually, if the partner who is the audience feels as though being an audience is becoming too much of a full-time pursuit, he or she may lose interest in serving in that role.

A second potential disadvantage is that humor can be used to see the light side of things, but it can also be used to be cruel in a passive-aggressive way. For example, the comedian may use humor to poke fun at the partner; the comedian is called on it by the partner; then the comedian explains that he or she was "only joking" and asks why the partner does not have a sense of humor. Of course, the partner may be too sensitive. But when humor is used as a means of demeaning a person in a way that is designed to protect the comedian from responsibility ("I was only joking"), a relationship is bound to be imperiled.

Finally, humor can be used as a way of bringing people together and of creating intimacy, or as a way of creating distance and thereby avoiding intimacy. It is thus an interesting example of something that in moderate amounts is good for a relationship, but in excessive amounts can be deleterious.

☞ THE MYSTERY STORY

In a mystery story, the mysterious aspects of a relationship predominate. Historically, romance has always been associated with an air of mystery.[1] Indeed, part of what makes the early stages of love so exciting is the air of mystery they carry. Each day may reveal new insights about one's partner. People with a mystery story hope never to see the end of this excitement. Most other people, on the other hand, expect the more mysterious aspects of their relationships to start to fade as the relationships begin to deepen and trust replaces mystery.

Diagnosing the Mystery Story

SLEUTH

1   I am often attracted to individuals who have an air of mystery about them.

2   I like it when my partner is a bit hard to figure out.

3   I often become attracted to individuals who are somewhat mysterious.

4   I find mysterious partners who have hidden secrets to be quite attractive.

MYSTERY FIGURE

1   I do not believe it is absolotely necessary to let my partner know a lot about m

2   I like to create a sense of mystery about myself in my close relationships.

3   I keep lots of secrets from my partner in my relationship and I like it that way.

4   I believe it is good to keep your partner guessing about yourself in a relationsh

---

Laura and Darrel

Laura has been seeing Darrel for six weeks, and for the most part things are going great. Not only is he attractive and intelligent, but he has a dynamic personality that makes it fun to be around him. She has only one worry: In the past, she has found that relationships in which she immediately reveals herself to her partner often end prematurely. Laura believes that love is all about getting to know someone better, and if you let too much of yourself be known right away, the relationship will experience burnout; there will be nothing left to discover. Because Laura has such strong feelings for Darrel, she does not want this burnout to occur. She wants to make sure that Darrel is constantly eager to figure out what she is all about. As a result, she hides much of herself, including many of her emotions, when she is around him.

Laura's behavior is having the precise effect on Darrel that she wanted it to. By concealing many of her emotions and several aspects of her life from him, Darrel is never exactly sure of what she is thinking or feeling. Although he is often frustrated by Laura's behavior, he enjoys the adventure of trying to unravel her mystery. He continually tries to get at what she is hiding from him, and although she occasionally reveals part of herself, she never offers him the whole story. For instance, Darrel frequently notices Laura scribbling something down on a piece of paper. When he asks her what she is writing, she will usually tell him that it is nothing, or that she is making a note of an errand she has to run.

Occasionally, however, when Laura feels like providing Darrel a reward for his efforts, she will tell him something about herself that he did not know: for example, that someday she would like to become a writer, and that when she writes something down it is usually an interesting phrase or idea that she would like to incorporate into a story. In so doing, she is obviously revealing a part of herself; however, she will not tell him that there is also a side of her that thinks there is something evil about putting her innermost feelings on paper and selling them to the public. Although Laura does not plan on keeping this information from Darrel forever, she believes that she should wait a little longer before discussing it with him.

Ordinarily Darrel believes that his adventurous quest to understand more about Laura will result in many interesting discoveries. But there are times when he wonders if maybe Laura really has nothing to hide, and that his efforts to figure her out are all for naught. He also realizes that she might possibly be hiding something from him that would cause him to change his opinion of her. Even without these concerns, Laura's obscurity often makes communication very difficult, especially when Darrel does not feel like playing sleuth and would rather just get to know her a little better. In addition, there are times when it seems as if what keeps their relationship going are his attempts to figure her out.

Fortunately, Laura is aware that Darrel might be having these doubts. She recognizes that she must continually reveal more and more of herself to him if she is to have any hope of the relationship succeeding over the long term. She is trying to strike a balance between keeping Darrel guessing and allowing him to discover new aspects of her. By doing so, Laura hopes to keep the relationship from becoming dull while at the same time developing a stronger, more intimate bond with him.

Martin and Jen

Martin and his best friend, Spencer, are having dinner at their favorite diner, but unfortunately, the mood is a somber one. Martin and his girlfriend, Jen, are having trouble with their relationship. Spencer is dumbfounded, because if Martin wanted to, he could easily resolve the difficulty that is plaguing his relationship. This difficulty can be summed up as Martin's refusal to reveal all of his feelings and emotions to Jen.

There will be many occasions when Jen will know that something is troubling Martin, but when she asks him to tell her what the matter is, he simply shrugs and says that everything is fine. His face, however, tells another story. Jen becomes very frustrated when Martin clams up, complaining that she will never get to know him if he continues to act so mysteriously around her.

Martin also hides certain facts of his life from Jen, the disclosure of which would make communication between them much easier. For instance, Jen paints for a living, and whenever she becomes depressed over an artistic block, she explains to Martin that he would not be able to understand what she is feeling because he is not an artist like her. She does not know that Martin is a wonderful painter, and has even had several of his paintings put on display at an art gallery.

Spencer finds scenarios like this one especially perplexing; he simply cannot figure out why Martin does not completely open up with Jen about his life and emotions. It seems to Spencer that Martin delights in keeping secrets, even ones that Jen would want to know about, such as Martin's painting skills. The two of them seem to love each other very much, and Martin's refusal to be candid with her about even basic things seems to be standing in the way of the further development of their relationship.

Their fight tonight began when Jen started to become suspicious that Martin's peculiar behavior might be a sign that he is hiding something serious from her, such as another relationship that he might be having. Martin could have firmly indicated that there is no such other relationship. But given the opportunity, he didn't take it.

Martin's explanation for his behavior revolves around his view of relationships. He believes that you should never completely reveal yourself to someone, and that the whole point of love is for your partner to try to discover who you are. He feels that if he were to tell Jen everything that there is to know about him, including all of his emotions and feelings at various times throughout the day, it would be like force-feeding a student the meaning of a particular book. The student might wind up knowing the facts of the book, as Jen might wind up knowing the facts about him, but neither would truly understand what these facts mean. To reach such understanding, Martin believes, you have to figure some things out for yourself.

It is for this reason that he has not even told Jen about his paintings. Certainly he could just tell her about them, and then Jen would be able to see that she could talk with him about her artistic blocks; however, Martin would prefer it if she could somehow figure out on her own that he is a painter, because her figuring it out for herself would show both of them that she has come to a deeper understanding of him. They would then be able to talk about their painting endeavors not merely as two distinct artists, but as two people who have a strong sense of what the other is all about.

Spencer agrees to a certain extent with what Martin is saying, but warns him that Jen might never be able to discover everything that there is to know about him. Martin realizes this fact, but maintains that if she makes an attempt to understand him better, she will certainly discover many things that as of yet she does not know. He adds that he does not think that this present fight will end their relationship. After all, Jen has told him on several occasions that she actually enjoys the adventure of trying to figure him out, and he believes that much of tonight's anger is a sign of the difficulty she is having in doing so. He recognizes, however, that he must promise Jen that his secrecy has nothing to do with another woman.

Modes of Thought and Behavior

People with a mystery story believe that mystery is an important component of love, and that one shouldn't let too much of oneself be known. At the very least, revelations should be gradual, and should not be made lightly. People with a mystery story tend to view themselves or others as having a lot of secrets, and prefer it that way.

The sleuthing aspect of love can, in fact, generate a lot of excitement. When you love someone, finding out about the individual is one of the most satisfying experiences you can have. People at the beginnings of relationships often act like an amateur Sherlock Holmes, paying attention to every detail in the words or behavior of their partner, hoping to extract from these details the mysteries of their loves. Typically, as time passes, the mystery aspect of a relationship starts to recede into the background. People with a mystery story want the mystery never to end.

Complementary Roles: Sleuth and Mystery Figure

The two complementary roles in the mystery story are the sleuth and the mystery figure. Although the roles may alternate, more commonly one person plays the sleuth, while the other is the mysterious stranger.

There can be something almost gothic about well-developed mystery stories, because many romance novels revolve around the unraveling of the mysteries that envelop one or the other partner in a relationship. On the other hand, there can also be something rather sad when, in well-developed relationships, a partner is withholding information that would be relevant and possibly even important for the other person to know.

Advantages and Disadvantages

The advantage of the mystery story is the excitement it generates. The mystery story turns a relationship into a continuing adventure in which one or both parties are trying to uncover interesting information about the other. Many people like mystery stories, and they can like mystery relationships for much the same reason—they maintain interest.

On the other hand, after one has read, say, ten mystery stories by the same author, things can start to become predictable. After a number of Perry Mason novels, for example, one gets the idea that the guilty party is usually the one who seems least to fit the role. Similarly, mystery stories in relationships can become predictable and therefore lose their mysterious character.

The mystery story can be used in a manipulative or even exploitative way, as when it is used to hide information that the other partner truly should know. One would scarcely want to be with a partner who has a serious, communicable disease, for example, under the pretense that the mystery of not knowing was part of the fun. For the partner who is kept in the dark, the fun of the mystery certainly does not justify the anxiety and hardship that the solution will bring when it is discovered.

The mystery story can also be used to hide the fact that a person has nothing to hide, and not much of anything to reveal, either. For example, Darrel has come to fear that maybe Laura uses mystery as a facade to hide shallowness. People can find themselves excited about learning the mysteries underlying another person, only to discover too late that there was never anything of real interest there in the first place.

III IMPLICATIONS

CAN WE CHANGE OUR STORIES AND IMPROVE OUR RELATIONSHIPS?

In this last part, I describe how the story view of love can help us improve our loving relationships.

TESTING THE STORY VIEW

Two years ago Karen realized that she was looking for "Mr. Goodbar," the proverbial destroyer in a horror story. She frequented singles bars, was involved in drugs, and found the most destructive men to be the most attractive. After being savagely beaten, her life was on a fast track—in a downward spiral. Then, one day, after Karen began to understand how her story was influencing her choices, and how she was reliving her mother's past life. Her mother had married an abusive and violent man, and now, in spite of her own protestations to the contrary, Karen was on the verge of doing the same thing. She hoped to relive the process, but change the ending, of her mother's life. Being severely beaten brought Karen to the realization that, if she didn't change, her ending would be no different than her mother's.

Casting off her old story has not been easy, but Karen now realizes that she was heading for disaster. When Karen meets a Mr. Goodbar type these days, she heads for the door. She still finds them tempting; however, it is a temptation she scrupulously tries to avoid.

Most "wish lists" that we carry around with us are not worth much. They are as likely to be based on what we feel we *should* want as on what we *really* want. But we can figure out what we really want only if we understand our ideal story, perhaps as revealed by scores on the love-story inventory scales contained for each story in this book. Even relationship books and guides are not optimally useful, because they list attributes people should look for if everyone were perfect and the same, rather than lists of what people actually want, based on who they are. To figure out what we want, we need to consider all of our past relationships. We need to ask ourselves what attributes the people to whom we feel most attracted have in common, and what attributes are shared by those to whom we were once attracted but are no longer. These attributes are different for different people.

Whether or not we are in the "looking" mode, understanding our ideal story will help us better understand what is not working in our relationship, and what we can do to make it work. Sometimes the ingredients are all there in our partner, and our old partner can come to be our new one. But to change our relationships fundamentally, we need to become conscious of our love stories and replot the endings.[1] We can become conscious of our stories by analyzing responses to the love-scale inventory items accompanying the stories in this book (although, of course, no inventory can represent *all* possible stories people might construct). Asking people what their stories are generally does not help, because people usually are not consciously aware of their stories.

If relationships become distressed, conventional efforts to change them are likely to fail if they do not take into account how our stories are unfolding in actual relationships. If we see our love stories as the dominating force in our relationships, what the couple believes to be the cause of the dissolution may actually be the effect. In other words, it is the story that gives rise to destructive behavior, rather than the behavior itself that is the cause of the dissolution. When relationships are nearing the breaking point, the decision actually to break off is often not mutual. After all, if things are so bad, why did the couple ever get together in the first place? How could things have started off so well and have ended up so poorly? And why is this course of events so common?

Again, the story view leads us away from focusing on behavior, and toward focusing on the stories through which behavior is interpreted. What matters is not only the action per se, but how it is interpreted through our stories and realized in the context in which we live.

Why would anyone tolerate extreme abuse or maltreatment, stories or no stories? From my point of view, it is because stories are so powerful in our lives, and also so hard to change. We may continue in a relationship that is dysfunctional in many respects simply because it does represent love to us, "sick" as that love may seem to others. We may even see the culture as supporting the kind of love we have. For example, the games of Richard Burton and Elizabeth Taylor in *Who's Afraid of Virginia Woolf?* may well have seemed sick to many of us, but they fulfilled the game story that both partners wanted in the relationship. Without the games, the characters and those who have this kind of story in real life would find themselves bored. The culture in which they lived allowed them the kind of story they had.

Once we understand the ideas behind the stories we accept as our own, we are in a position to do some replotting. We can ask ourselves what we like and don't like about our current (or past) story, and how we would like to change it. We then ask ourselves what we could do to replot the story. Replotting may involve changing stories, or transforming an existing story to make it more adaptive. For example, "horror" stories may be fantasized during sexual or other activity, rather than actually physically played out. In replotting, we need to recognize our own background factors that affect how we plot and set the themes for our stories. We also have to understand the cultural context in which we live. At the same time, we need to understand our partner's story and how he or she would like it to change. The inventory items in this book may be helpful, then, to both partners in deciding their stories, and in serving as one basis for deciding where things are and where they need to go.

Sometimes we need to get outside our own or our partner's story temporarily in order to understand it better. We get outside the story when we analyze it, as is done in this book, in addition to living the story uncritically. Thus, repairing relationships requires more than rational lists. It requires storytelling. We often need to try out new stories piece by piece, discovering which stories can work for us and which cannot. Sometimes we need to let others help us replot our stories, rather than going it on our own. Consider the case of Louise and John.

Louise and John have been committed to improving their relationship for a long time. They tried books, they tried counseling, and they tried encounter groups. Nothing seemed to work. Then, almost by chance, Louise told John a fable. It was one she made up about a prince and a princess who defied all expectations—they didn't live happily ever after. Of course, the story was about Louise and John. John replied, several days later, with a story of his own. It was about a prince and a princess who did live happily ever after, following a period of discontent. The story exchange continued. It enabled both Louise and John to understand their stories, without direct confrontation, without threat, without anxiety. Soon they started trying to live the story they created that they liked. Today they are living this story. They are the prince and princess who are living happily ever after.

We don't always need to be rational. Relationships at their core are not rational: They are stories. Accepting this fact means moving away from notions of who's right and who's wrong, and toward notions of understanding and changing stories that are neither right nor wrong, but very, very real. We can understand and change relationships only if we accept them for what they are, rather than what some might wish them to be in a hypothetical world.

Does the story view hold up to empirical tests? In a test of the view of love as a story, Laurie Lynch and I constructed a seventy-five-item questionnaire that was intended to measure the extent to which each of twenty-five stories characterized people's own views of love.[2] There were three statements for each of the stories (e.g., "Relationships are fun when one person is actually frightened of the other" [horror], "When all is said and done, economic considerations are of key importance to a relationship" [business], and "I tend to end up with people who need help getting over bad histories or habits" [recovery]). The statements presented with each of the stories in this book are from an updated version of this questionnaire.

Participants in this study rated each of the statements on a 1 ("strongly disagree") to 7 ("strongly agree") scale, where 4 was the intermediate value ("I neither agree nor disagree"). (In later work, we have switched to a 1 to 9 scale.) Each statement was rated twice: once for the actual relationship in which the person was participating and once for the ideal relationship the person would hope to have. Participants also received a demographic questionnaire and a relationship-satisfaction questionnaire.

Sixty undergraduates, half male and half female, ranging in age from seventeen to twenty-two years (mean age 18.8 years), participated in the small study. All had to have been in at least one intimate relationship (past or present).

Of the twenty-five story scales for actual relationships that we used in this study, four showed a significant sex difference: art, collectibles, and pornography (all with males higher), and travel (with women higher). There were also large overall differences in average rated values, with horror the lowest (1.56) and gardening the highest (5.68). For ideal relationships, men rated art, collectibles, and pornography higher, and women rated business higher. Overall average rated values were also lowest for horror and highest for gardening, meaning that the horror story was the least popular and the gardening story the most popular.

In another study, with forty-three couples, Mahzad Hojjat and I found that men were more likely than women to have art, pornography, and (to our surprise) sacrifice stories. Thus, there was some tendency for men to be more likely than women to treat their partners as objects, but there was also a willingness by some men to sacrifice for their relationship. Women were more likely to have travel stories. Couples had similar profiles of stories; that is, partners were generally compatible in terms of their story preferences. As the theory predicts, then, people tend to end up with partners sharing similar profiles of stories. Certain stories tended to be associated with lower satisfaction in close relationships: business, collection, (autocratic) government, horror, mystery, police, recovery, science fiction, and theater. None of the stories guaranteed happiness: Stories can facilitate happiness, but compatible stories facilitate happiness without guaranteeing it. Most important of all, the more discrepant the profiles of stories of the couple were, the less happy the couple was in the relationship.

In yet another study, with fifty-five couples, Hojjat and I found that if we were to distinguish two broad kinds of stories, they would be ones where power either is equal or unequal. People getting into relationships need to be sensitive early on to the power distribution in a relationship, because once it starts to be set, it is difficult to change.

We concluded from our research that the love-is-a-story view is useful for explaining why people are attracted to some individuals and not to others, and why some relationships endure whereas others fail. It also suggests that even relationships that seem distressed to outsiders may last if the stories are compatible for the people in the relationships, and relationships that seem to outsiders to be working may end if the stories are not compatible for the people involved. In general, the extent to which people will experience lasting love will depend on the extent to which partners can fulfill the roles in each other's stories.

WHAT IS LOVE?

There is no magic bullet to making love better—that should be clear by now. Books about the seven steps to a better relationship, or whatever they are called, are likely only to work for those people who view their relationship as a cookbook story and thus want to and really can follow a recipe, or for those who genuinely want to try a recipe from someone else. For the most part, though, there cannot be a magic bullet that works for everyone, because people have such diverse stories of love.

These stories are not limited to the twenty-five described in this volume. First, the potential number of stories is infinite, including but not limited to blends of the stories described here. Second, people have a hierarchy of stories, meaning that they probably are drawn to multiple stories at once. Third, people's stories can change throughout their lifetimes. And fourth, even when the stories stay the same, they keep being written throughout each person's life. Stories are constantly in a state of development.

Nevertheless, the story view has some implications for making love better. They are not how-to implications, but ways of reconceptualizing what love is about and how it can be made more satisfying. At the same time, it is important to remember that in close relationships, love is part, but not all, of what leads to success.[1] A supportive environment, friendships, economic well-being, spiritual fulfillment, and compatible interests and values all make a difference, too.

• *Understanding and appreciating the role of stories in love*. If people understand the role stories play in love, then they are already in a good position to improve their relationships. Most people, oblivious to the role stories play, keep making the same mistakes again and again, unwittingly repeating whatever maladaptive thoughts, feelings, and actions their stories generate. Knowing the role of stories helps people realize that all stories can have both good and bad elements, and that people need to find a way to make the most of the good and to compensate for or try to reduce the impact of the bad.

• *Inferring one's own hierarchy of stories*. There are several ways people can infer their own hierarchy of stories, and thereby understand themselves better.

One way to infer your own hierarchy of stories is to think about the questions posed in this book, and evaluate your own profile of scores.

A second way to infer a hierarchy of stories is to think about the kinds of people who appeal to you and the kinds of events that happen in your relationships with these people. What kinds of stories do these people and events play into?

In some of my research with Mahzad Hojjat, we simply asked people to tell stories of their love relationships. When we did this, the stories we received were rather superficial, dwelling on surface events such as when the two people met and the kinds of things the people like to do together. In order to infer your own stories, you need to concentrate on what these events have meant to you, not just on what they are objectively.

A third way you can infer your stories is by asking yourself what kinds of stories about love appeal to you in books, television, or the movies. Although the media probably do not represent all the stories described in this book, they do represent some of them. Because people tend to project their own feelings onto those of characters in stories, the kinds of stories people like in the media can provide at least a hint of the kinds of stories people like in their own lives.

A fourth way you can infer your stories is to ask others about their perceptions of you. Often others can see things in the way you think and act that you cannot see yourself.

- *Inferring the story hierarchy of your partner.* It is at least as important to understand your partner's hierarchy of stories as it is to understand your own. The techniques described above can be applied to partners as well as yourself. Your own judgment of your partner's hierarchy of stories may be as useful as the partner's judgment.

- *Considering the match between your ideal stories and the story you are in.* People have a hierarchy of ideal stories as well as the actual story they find themselves in. By comparing the ideal story hierarchy to one's actual story and deciding how close they are to a match, people can reflect on whether a relationship or potential relationship has the right story for them.

- *Trying to maximize the adaptive characteristics of stories and to minimize the maladaptive ones.* The descriptions of the various stories included characterizations of some of the advantages and disadvantages of each story. By being aware of the advantages and disadvantages, people can try to make the best of the stories they have.

- *Realizing that although stories guide how we select our partners and maintain our relationships, they do not control the relationship or our partners.* Ultimately, it is within a person's own power to decide whom he or she will pursue as a potential partner in love, and with whom he or she will maintain a relationship. Stories can only shape people's perceptions of relationships and guide people's relationships; the decisions are theirs to make. People may, for example, find that the horror story exerts a strong pull on them, but they may nevertheless choose not to pursue such a story.

- *Understanding that stories influence both the events that occur in relationships and the interpretations of those events.* People tend to view both events and their interpretations as givens. They usually assume that the events occur more or less on their own, and that there is a correct interpretation of these events—usually their own interpretation. An implication of the story view is that we actively shape events in our relationships to realize our stories, and that we interpret the meanings of the events in terms of these stories. Realize that these interpretations are subjective, and may not correspond to our partner's interpretation of the same events. There is no one "right" interpretation of events, or at least none that we can know. Thus, it is important to understand things from both your own and your partner's point of view.

• *Realizing that stories are constantly being written and rewritten.* One's story does not end when one turns eighteen, or twenty-one, or fifty, or eighty. We are constantly writing the story of our relationship as the relationship progresses. Even after a relationship ends, we may rewrite the story several times, so that the account we give ourselves and others five or ten years after the relationship has ended may be quite different from the account we wrote right after it ended. In interpreting your own as well as others' stories, therefore, it is important to realize that they are never final, but works in progress. As such, they are subject to change, even after relationships terminate.

• *Appreciating that within a given kind of story, there is room for great variation.* There is not just one way in which a given kind of story can be written. For example, there are an infinite number of variations on the cookbook story; different recipes work for different cookbook relationships, and sometimes the recipe changes even over the course of the relationship. Similarly, there are an infinite number of variations of the travel story; there is no end to the destinations a couple can pick, nor of the routes to getting to these destinations. Indeed, every kind of story has infinite variations. Thus, even if you strongly favor one kind of story, all kinds of variations are possible within it. And because we are constantly writing, we can start these variations at any given time.

• *Understanding that stories are hard but not impossible to change.* Stories are difficult to change, but people change them all the time. Because every story has its pluses and minuses, by focusing on the pluses of certain stories that we find more adaptive, and the minuses of those we find less adaptive, we can tilt ourselves toward the stories that work best for us. And if this effort does not succeed, good psychotherapy can help us find stories that are more adaptive than the ones we currently have.

That love is a story closes off no options to us; instead, it makes us aware of the infinite options we can create as we write the stories of our lives and loves.

NOTES

PREFACE
1. Robert J. Sternberg and Susan Grajek, "The Nature of Love," *Journal of Personality and Social Psychology* 47 (1984): 312–29.
2. Robert J. Sternberg, "A Triangular Theory of Love," *Psychological Review* 93 (1986): 119–35; Robert J. Sternberg, *The Triangle of Love* (New York: Basic Books, 1988).
3. Robert J. Sternberg, "Love Is a Story," *The General Psychologist* 30, no. 1 (1994): 1–11; Robert J. Sternberg, "Love as a Story," *Journal of Social and Personal Relationships* 12 (1995): 541–46; Robert J. Sternberg, "Love Stories," *Personal Relationships* 3 (1996): 1359–79.
4. Anne E. Beall and Robert J. Sternberg, "The Social Construction of Love," *Journal of Social and Personal Relationships* 12 (1995): 417–38.

LOVE AS A STORY
1. Robert J. Sternberg, "Love Is a Story," *The General Psychologist* 30, no. 1 (1994): 1–11; Robert J. Sternberg, "Love as a Story," *Journal of Social and Personal Relationships* 12 (1995): 541–46; Robert J. Sternberg, "Love Stories," *Personal Relationships* 3 (1996): 1359–79.
2. Sternberg, "Love Stories." See also B. J. Cohler, "Personal Narrative and the Life Course," in *Life Span Development and Behavior*, ed. Paul Baltes and Orville Brim Jr. (New York: Academic Press, 1979), vol. 4, pp. 205–41; R. Josselson and A. Lieblich (eds.), *The Narrative Study of Lives* (Newbury Park, CA: Sage, 1982); S. L. Murray and J. G. Holmes, "Storytelling in Close Relationships: The Construction of Confidence," *Personality and Social Psychology Bulletin* 20 (1994): 650–63; T. Sarbin (ed.), *Narrative Psychology: The Storied Nature of Human Conduct* (New York: Praeger, 1986).
3. Robert J. Sternberg and Michael L. Barnes, "Real and Ideal Others in Romantic Relationships," *Journal of Personality and Social Psychology* 49 (1985): 1586–1608.

OUR MULTIPLE STORIES OF LOVE
1. Stanley Coren, Lawrence M. Ward, and James T. Enns, *Sensation and Perception*, 4th ed. (Ft. Worth, TX: Harcourt Brace College Publishers, 1994).

STORY ELEMENTS
1. Seymour Epstein and Archie Brodsky, *You're Smarter Than You Think* (New York: Simon and Schuster, 1993).

SOME KINDS OF STORIES
1. Aaron T. Beck, *Love Is Never Enough* (New York: Harper and Row, 1988).

WHERE DO STORIES COME FROM, AND WHERE CAN THEY GO?
1. Jeffrey E. Young and Janet S. Klosko, *Reinventing Your Life* (New York: Dutton, 1993).
2. Dan P. McAdams, *Stories We Live By* (New York: Morrow, 1993); Diane Wolkstein, *The First Love Stories* (New York: HarperCollins, 1991).
3. Richard E. Nisbett and Lee Ross, *Human Inference: Strategies and Shortcomings of Social Judgment* (Englewood Cliffs, NJ: Prentice-Hall, 1980).
4. Lee Ross, "The Intuitive Psychologist and His Shortcomings: Distortions in the Attribution Process," in *Advances in Experimental Social Psychology*, ed. Leonard Berkowitz (New York: Academic Press, 1977), vol. 10.
5. Robert J. Sternberg and Michael L. Barnes, "Real and Ideal Others in Romantic Relationships," *Journal of Personality and Social Psychology* 49 (1985): 1586–1608.
6. Ellen Berscheid, "Emotion," in *Close Relationships*, ed. H. H. Kelley et al. (New York: W. H. Freeman, 1983), pp. 110–68; Ellen Berscheid, "Interpersonal Relationships," *Annual Review of Psychology* 45 (1994): 79–129; G. Mandler, "The Generation of Emotion: A Psychological Theory," in *Emotion: Theory, Research, and Experience*, vol. 1: *Theories of Emotion,* ed. R. Plutchik and H. Kellerman (New York: Academic Press, 1980), pp. 219–43.
7. Arthur Aron and Lori Westbay, "Dimensions of the Prototype of Love," *Journal of Personality and Social Psychology* 70 (1996): 535–51; Michael L. Barnes and Robert J. Sternberg, "A Hierarchical Model of Love and Its Prediction of Satisfaction in Close Relationships," in *Satisfaction in Close Relationships,* ed. Robert J. Sternberg and Mahzad Hojjat (New York: Guilford, 1997), pp. 79–101; Beverly Fehr, "Prototype Analysis of the Concepts of Love and Commitment," *Journal of Personality and Social Psychology* 55 (1988): 557–79; Beverly Fehr and James A. Russell, "The Concept of Love Viewed from a Prototype Perspective," *Journal of Personality and Social Psychology* 60 (1991): 425–35.
8. Diane Ackerman, *A Natural History of Love* (New York: Random House, 1994); Kenneth L. Dion and Karen K. Dion, "Cultural Perspectives on Romantic Love," *Personal Relationships* 3 (1996): 5–17; Morton M. Hunt, *The Natural History of Love* (New York: Knopf, 1959); Irving Singer, *The Nature of Love*, 3 vols., 2nd ed. (Chicago: University of Chicago Press, 1984).
9. Dan P. McAdams, *Stories We Live By* (New York: Morrow, 1993).

ASYMMETRICAL STORIES

The Teacher-Student Story
1. Thomas N. Bradbury and Frank D. Fincham, "Attributions in Marriage: Review and Critique," *Psychological Bulletin* 107 (1990): 3–33.

The Sacrifice Story
1. John Alan Lee, *Colors of Love* (Toronto: New Press, 1973).
2. Elaine Walster, G. W. Walster, and Ellen Berscheid, *Equity: Theory and Research* (Boston: Allyn and Bacon, 1978).
3. Judson Mills and Margaret S. Clark, "Communal and Exchange Relationships: Controversies and Research," in *Theoretical Frameworks for Personal Relationships*, ed. R.

Erber and Robin Gilmour (Hillsdale, NJ: Lawrence Erlbaum Associates, 1994), pp. 29–42.

The Government Story
1. Henry A. Murray, *Explorations in Personality* (New York: Oxford University Press, 1938).
2. Ibid.
3. Ted L. Huston, "Power," in *Close Relationships,* ed. Harold Kelley et al. (New York: W. H. Freeman, 1983), pp. 169–219.

The Police Story
1. Philip G. Zimbardo, "Psychology of Imprisonment," *Transition/Society*, 9(6) (1972): 4–8.

The Pornography Story
1. Robert J. Sternberg, "Love Stories," *Personal Relationships* 3 (1996): 1359–79.

The Horror Story
1. Albert Bandura, *Aggression: A Social Learning Analysis* (Englewood Cliffs, NJ: Prentice-Hall, 1973); Albert Bandura, *Social Learning Theory* (Englewood Cliffs, NJ: Prentice-Hall, 1977).
2. Henry A. Murray, *Explorations in Personality* (New York: Oxford University Press, 1938).
3. Stanley Milgram, *Obedience to Authority: An Experimental View* (New York: Harper and Row, 1974).
4. Walter Mischel and Y. Shoda, "A Cognitive-Affective System Theory of Personality: Reconceptualizing Situations, Dispositions, Dynamics, and Invariance in Personality Structure," *Psychological Review* 102 (1995): 246–68.

OBJECT STORIES

The Science-Fiction Story
1. Patricia Noller and M. Ruzzene, "Communication in Marriage: The Influence of Affect and Cognition," in *Cognition and Close Relationships,* ed. Garth J. O. Fletcher and Frank D. Fincham (Hillsdale, NJ: Lawrence Erlbaum Associates, 1991), pp. 203–34.

The Collection Story
1. Jack W. Brehm, *A Theory of Psychological Reactance* (New York: Academic Press, 1966); Sharon S. Brehm and Jack W. Brehm, *Psychological Reactance: A Theory of Freedom and Control* (New York: Academic Press, 1981).
2. Cynthia Hazan and Phillip R. Shaver, "Romantic Love Conceptualized as an Attachment Process," *Journal of Personality and Social Psychology* 52 (1987): 511–24; Phillip R. Shaver and Cynthia Hazan, "Adult Romantic Attachment: Theory and Evidence," in *Advances in Personal Relationships,* ed. Warren H. Jones and Daniel Perlman (London: Jessica Kingsley, 1987), vol. 4, pp. 29–70; Phillip R. Shaver, Cynthia Hazan, and Donna Bradshaw, "Love as Attachment: The Integration of Three Behavioral Systems," in *The Psychology of Love,* ed. Robert J. Sternberg and Michael L. Barnes (New Haven, CT: Yale University Press), pp. 68–99.

The Art Story
1. David M. Buss, *The Evolution of Desire: Strategies of Human Mating* (New York: Basic Books, 1994); Helen E. Fisher, *Anatomy of Love* (New York: Norton, 1992); Mer-

edith F. Small, *What's Love Got to Do with It?* (New York: Anchor Books, 1995); Glenn Wilson, *The Coolidge Effect* (New York: Morrow, 1981).

2. Judith H. Langlois and L. A. Roggman, "Attractive Faces Are Only Average," *Psychological Science* 1 (1990): 115–21.

3. Ibid.

4. Elaine Hatfield and Susan Sprecher, *Mirror, Mirror: The Importance of Looks in Everyday Life* (Albany, NY: State University of New York Press, 1986).

5. Mark Snyder, E. D. Tanke, and Ellen Berscheid, "Social Perception and Interpersonal Behavior: On the Self-Fulfilling Nature of Social Stereotypes," *Journal of Personality and Social Psychology* 35 (1977): 656–66.

The House and Home Story
1. Albert J. Lott and Bernice E. Lott, "A Learning Theory Approach to Interpersonal Attitudes," in *Psychological Foundations of Attitudes,* ed. Anthony G. Greenwald and Thomas M. Ostrom (New York: Academic Press, 1968), pp. 67–88; Gerald L. Clore and Donn Byrne, "A Reinforcement-Affect Model of Attraction," in *Foundations of Interpersonal Attraction,* ed. Ted L. Huston (New York: Academic Press, 1974), pp. 143–70.

The Recovery Story
1. Abraham H. Maslow, *Motivation and Personality* (New York: Harper and Row, 1954).

The Religion Story
1. Theodore Reik, *A Psychologist Looks at Love* (New York: Holt, Rinehart & Winston, 1944).

The Game Story
1. Ovid (Publius Ovidius Naso), *The Erotic Poems,* trans. Peter Green (New York: Penguin, 1982).

2. John Alan Lee, *Colors of Love* (Toronto: New Press, 1973).

3. R. Duncan Luce and Howard Raiffa, *Games and Decisions* (New York: Wiley, 1957).

4. Judson Mills and Margaret S. Clark, "Communal and Exchange Relationships: Controversies and Research," in *Theoretical Frameworks for Personal Relationships*, ed. R. Erber and Robin Gilmour (Hillsdale, NJ: Lawrence Erlbaum Associates, 1994), pp. 29–42.

COORDINATION STORIES

The Travel Story
1. Diane Wolkstein, *The First Love Stories* (New York: HarperCollins, 1991).

The Sewing and Knitting Story
1. Anne E. Beall and Robert J. Sternberg, "The Social Construction of Love," *Journal of Social and Personal Relationships* 12 (1995): 417–38.

The Garden Story
1. Elaine Hatfield, "Passionate and Companionate Love," in *The Psychology of Love,* ed. Robert J. Sternberg and Michael L. Barnes (New Haven, CT: Yale University Press, 1988), pp. 191–217.

2. John Alan Lee, *Colors of Love* (Toronto: New Press, 1973).

The Business Story

1. John Alan Lee, "Love-Styles," in *The Psychology of Love*, ed. Robert J. Sternberg and Michael L. Barnes (New Haven, CT: Yale University Press, 1988), pp. 38–67. See also Clyde Hendrick and Susan S. Hendrick, "A Theory and Method of Love," *Journal of Personality and Social Psychology* 50 (1986): 392–402.

2. Elaine Hatfield, "Passionate and Companionate Love," in *The Psychology of Love*, ed. Robert J. Sternberg and Michael L. Barnes (New Haven, CT: Yale University Press, 1988), pp. 191–217; Elaine Hatfield and Richard L. Rapson, *Love, Sex, and Intimacy: Their Psychology, Biology, and History* (New York: HarperCollins, 1993).

The Addiction Story

1. Stanton Peele, "Fools for Love: The Romantic Ideal, Psychological Theory, and Addictive Love," in *The Psychology of Love*, ed. Robert J. Sternberg and Michael L. Barnes (New Haven, CT: Yale University Press, 1988), pp. 159–88; Stanton Peele and A. Brodsky, *Love and Addiction* (New York: New American Library, 1976).

2. Robert J. Sternberg, *The Triangle of Love* (New York: Basic Books, 1988).

3. Richard L. Solomon, "The Opponent-Process Theory of Acquired Motivation: The Costs of Pleasure and the Benefits of Pain," *American Psychologist* 35 (1980): 691–712.

NARRATIVE STORIES

The Fantasy Story

1. Diane Wolkstein, *The First Love Stories* (New York: HarperCollins, 1991); see also Robert J. Sternberg, *In Search of the Human Mind* (Ft. Worth, TX: Harcourt Brace College Publishers, 1995).

2. Francesco Alberoni, *Falling in Love* (New York: Random House, 1983).

3. Anne E. Beall and Robert J. Sternberg, "Love and Science: Can the Two Be Married?" *Journal of NIH Research* 2 (1990): 57–61; Robert J. Sternberg and Michael L. Barnes, "Real and Ideal Others in Romantic Relationships," *Journal of Personality and Social Psychology* 49 (1985): 1586–1608.

The History Story

1. Robert J. Sternberg and Elena L. Grigorenko (eds.), *Intelligence, Heredity, and Environment* (New York: Cambridge University Press, 1997).

The Science Story

1. Howard Gardner, Mindy L. Kornhaber, and Warren K. Wake, *Intelligence: Multiple Perspectives* (Ft. Worth, TX: Harcourt Brace College Publishers, 1996); Robert J. Sternberg, *Successful Intelligence* (New York: Simon and Schuster, 1996).

2. Howard Gardner, *Frames of Mind: The Theory of Multiple Intelligences* (New York: Basic Books, 1983).

The Cookbook Story

1. Robert J. Sternberg with Catherine Whitney, *Love the Way You Want It* (New York: Bantam, 1991); see also Robert J. Sternberg, *Cognitive Psychology* (Ft. Worth, TX: Harcourt Brace College Publishers, 1996).

2. Robert J. Sternberg, *Successful Intelligence* (New York: Simon and Schuster, 1996); Robert J. Sternberg and Louise Spear-Swerling, *Teaching for Thinking* (Washington, DC: American Psychological Association, 1996).

3. Robert J. Sternberg, *Thinking Styles* (New York: Cambridge University Press, 1997).

GENRE STORIES

The War Story
1. John M. Gottman, *What Predicts Divorce? The Relationships between Marital Processes and Marital Outcomes* (Hillsdale, NJ: Lawrence Erlbaum Associates, 1994); Howard J. Markman, "Prediction of Marital Distress: A Five-Year Follow-Up," *Journal of Consulting and Clinical Psychology* 49 (1981): 760–62.

The Theater Story
1. Erving Goffman, *The Presentation of Self in Everyday Life* (Garden City, NY: Doubleday, 1959); Roger C. Schank and Robert P. Abelson, *Scripts, Plans, Goals, and Understanding* (Hillsdale, NJ: Lawrence Erlbaum Associates, 1977).

The Humor Story
1. John H. Harvey, *Odyssey of the Heart: The Search for Closeness, Intimacy, and Love* (New York: W. H. Freeman, 1995); George Levinger and H. L. Raush (eds.), *Close Relationships: Perspectives on the Meaning of Intimacy* (Amherst, MA: University of Massachusetts Press, 1977); Harry T. Reis, "The Role of Intimacy in Interpersonal Relations," *Journal of Social and Clinical Psychology* 9 (1990): 15–30.

The Mystery Story
1. Denis De Rougemont, *Love in the Western World* (New York: Random House, 1983).

TESTING THE STORY VIEW
1. Robert J. Sternberg, "Love Stories," *Personal Relationships* 3 (1996): 1359–79.
2. Patricia O'Hanlon Hudson and William Hudson O'Hanlon, *Rewriting Love Stories* (New York: Norton, 1991).

WHAT IS LOVE?
1. Aaron T. Beck, *Love Is Never Enough* (New York: Harper and Row, 1988); Robert J. Sternberg, *The Triangle of Love* (New York: Basic Books, 1988); Robert J. Sternberg, "Triangulating Love," in *The Psychology of Love,* ed. Robert J. Sternberg and Michael L. Barnes (New Haven, CT: Yale University Press, 1988), pp. 119–38; Robert J. Sternberg, "What's Love Got to Do With It?" *Omni* 10 (1988): 27.

⟿ INDEX